THE VASE OF SUSO
and the Lost Scrolls of 'J'

Also by Ivan Kireevskii

The Vase of Suso

and the Lost Scrolls of 'J'

IVAN KIREEVSKII

LUMINARE PRESS

WWW.LUMINAREPRESS.COM

The Vase of Suso and the Lost Scrolls of 'J'
Copyright © 2021 by Ivan Kireevskii

Printed in the United States of America

Luminare Press
442 Charnelton St.
Eugene, OR 97401
www.luminarepress.com

LCCN: 2021911310
ISBN: 978-1-64388-755-5

FOR MY DAUGHTERS
Heather, Wendy, Robin, Candice and Sarah

CONTENTS

Preface

IN IVAN KIREEVSKII'S MOST AMBITIOUS WORK TO DATE, through an epic poem he journey's deep into the thoughts, words and teachings of some of history's most celebrated teachers, prophets, poets, story-tellers and mystics.

Have you ever wondered what a dialogue between Nagarjuna, Nietzsche, Jesus, William Blake, Charles Darwin and the mysterious unknown author, known as the "J" writer would be like?

What mysteries would they present to us? In a series of poetic exchanges, Kireevskii lets them take us into the deepest mysteries of life, as they present their views of the contents of the "J" writer's lost scrolls.

Throughout this adventure, Suso is presented with the sage counsel of these seers, searching not only for the contents of 'J's lost scroll but for answers to questions that have haunted him since his days as a young child.

Walking forward, mental images of an unknown world explode before him. Uncertain whether the scenes are real or imaginary... as a set of distinct yet mutually interdependent motifs, woven together, form a magic tapestry that is displayed before Suso.

This is a philosophical poem and no doubt, at times, very difficult to understand. But the readers patience and endurance will be richly rewarded. Many of the ideas and images were influenced by a deep desire to understand the inner life of man.

There is much symbolic interpretation of natural phenomenon here as Kireevskii's poetic imagination penetrates the secrets of even the structure of matter.

An interpreter might very well hesitate in such a writing, conflicted between taking the author for a madman or imputing him to a nearly Swiftian taste for fantastic parable, while the truth is, he may sense something else altogether, but what?

If man is so important, then his inner life cannot be just a kind of vapor, of no consequence when compared to tangible phenomena, rather must have a cosmic meaning. Here Kireevskii introduces a new dimension of human interiority, paralleling what contemporaries might consider as categories within the mind; the literal, the spiritual and the celestial. Read with this in mind, this epic loses its contradictions.

This approach favors the poet's intricate structure; in fact, leaving the reader grasping at something that eludes him right up to the last moment. This includes the personification of forces, conforming a cosmic dimension of man as opposed to his diminutive size in the material universe.

It is the hope of this poet, that this magic tapestry will be spread before you, dear reader as well.

—PATRICIA MARSHALL
Publisher, Luminare Press

$\mathcal{C}$HARACTER
DESCRIPTIVE NOTES

THE FOLLOWING HISTORICAL INDIVIDUALS HAVE BEEN fictionalized in this epic poem. Below are the names they are given in the story. Where it differs from their actual identity, it is noted in below:

Ashu: Ashu Zarathustra is the sage and prophet of Nietzsche's philosophical-literary masterpiece, *Thus Spake Zarathustra*. Often in this book, the views of Zarathustra and Nietzsche are interchangeable.

Devil's Chaplain: The description Charles Darwin gave of himself in reference to his book; *The Origin of Species,* where he introduced the theory of evolution by natural selection.

Issa: According to a document uncovered in Ladakh, Jesus abandoned Jerusalem at the age of 13 and set out towards Sind, intending to improve and perfect himself in the divine understanding, he set out to study the Vedas under Brahmin priests. He spent time in Tibetan monasteries, studying Buddhism and returned to Jerusalem at the age of 29.

"J": J is the title that scholars ascribe to the nameless writer they believe is responsible for the text, written between

950 and 900 BCE, on which the Old Testament books of *Genesis, Exodus* and *Numbers* are based.

Los: The "eternal prophet" and divine aspect of the imagination in the mythological writings of William Blake's 1795 book, *The Book of Los.*

Nagarjuna: Second century Indian Buddhist philosopher who articulated the doctrine of emptiness (*shunyata*) and is traditionally regarded as the founder of the Madhyamika ("Middle Way") school, an important tradition of Mahayana Buddhist philosophy.

Suso: A fourteenth century mystic who called himself the "servant of Eternal Wisdom," he endured long stretches of spiritual darkness interrupted only by occasional bursts of brightness.

I am not a man or a poet or a leaf
but a wounded pulse that probes the things of the other side.

—Federico García Lorca

Will the writings of Berkeley and of Blake together with those works which inspired their thought be among the sacred books, perhaps, of an age in which not matter but mind will again be the theme of philosopher and poet?

…a voice Soft as the rustle of a seed from Cloyne That gathers volume; now a thunder-clap.

—RAINE, KATHLEEN,
BLAKE AND THE NEW AGE

Prologue

Suso enters the chamber dressed in a magnificently adorned bishop's style black cassock trimmed in purple, a short mozetta cape draped across his back, wearing a tall double pointed mitre on his head and cross of gold suspended around his neck.

He is escorted by two beautiful young women dressed in long white flowing gowns… the gowns cover their slender, yet perfectly shaped bodies as if by soft white clouds.

Protruding from their gowns of clouds, as if attached to their shoulders, the appearance of tall wings stretching heavenward.

Suso is prominently taken to what appears to be a throne. As he is seated, the beautiful young women take their stance… now appearing as angels at guard at his east and west side.

Suso gazes across the chamber to an open window where he witnesses a breathtaking waterfall, a bright purple sunset… the backgound for a quiet view of a garden of Juliet Roses, Fire Lilies and Queens of the Night, Kadupuls.

Suso's mind drifts back in time. A time when he as a young boy was escorted to church each Sunday morning. As if reading his mind, his angelic guards open their arms wide and raise their hands heavenward.

I

i walked to church
father grabbed my hand
mama sang the moment
i absorbed the meaning

i, the enlightened one
when heaven was young

lined in orderly patterns
everything understood
it was all explained to me
i absorbed the meaning

i the enlightened one
when heaven was young

The angel on his east rose and for a brief moment and
departed from his side, only to return
with an amphora vase… first appearing filled with
handpicked *queens of night* that then became pages of
handpicked verses that filled this vase.

queens of the night
verses divine
once lined in orderly patterns
what was once understood
now was changing
in kaleidoscopic motion

i the enlightened one
when heaven was young

but suddenly there was the sound of haunting music
of shaken confidence…
shrouded in its newness
the newness of doubt

pater naster, qui es in caelis
take heed that no man deceive you

sanctificatur nomen tuum
wherefore if they shall say unto you
behold, he is in the desert
go not forth

adveniat regnum tuum
behold, he is in the secret chamber
believe it not

the beautiful angels
step before him to delicately remove the mitre
the gold cross
and the mozetta cape

he now stands, as if alone

wearing only his simple black cassock
he steps forward
attempts to reach inside the vase

the angels are no longer poised
arms no longer raised heavenward
they remove the vase from his grasp
suso at once felt a stillness upon him

and he once again drifts back in time
but this time things felt different…

blindness eclipsed the valley
at this moment
at this crossroad of perfection
i lit the candles
i placed incense at their feet

bowed in acquiescence
absolved in life's water

i absorbed the meaning
i, the enlightened one
when heaven was young

fiat voluntas tua
the sun shall be darkened

sicut in caelo et in terra
the moon shall not give her light

then the angels delicately remove the black cassock

suso now stands
dressed in simple black

the angels return
they stand stiff and motionless at his side

and then the evening
and then the morning

i reached out to the ancients
their motifs crashed in upon my soul
i absorbed the meaning
i, the enlightened one
when heaven was young

suso slowly walks
as if half searching
half exploring
still dressed in black… however
upon close examination
he is now barefoot

images explode across his mind
as he walks…
an unknown world explodes before him

are these scenes real
or is he imagining

Panem nostrum quotidianum

the moon is bright
the stars are shining off in the distance

suso walks to the sea
where he stares into the heavens
with a feeling of uncontrollable confusion

he lays down in the sand and falls asleep

in the pebbles of the holy streams
the leaping saga of prayer
and high there on the hare-heeled winds
are the rooks
and the holy books

da nobis hodie

thou art like a hare hiding
frightened by the whispering of the leaves

thou art frightened every day
by the griefs that come to thee

he is swept into the wounds
and cries
he climbs to greet this war within
in which there is no heart

suso is suffering acutely
a mountain weighs on his heart
this bewildered lover of eternal wisdom
suffering acutely

an inner voice mocked his weakness
the secret mortifications
his selfhood is stripped away
crushed and wounded
to the depths of his broken heart

suso's feeble nature has been broken
by the pains which he had to endure

leading him forth
raving like one who has lost his senses
he hides himself
in a place far from men

while the bristling flowers
murder his moses
and close to the rushes of his heaven
where his once sea of calm
held him safely

but now, as if tied to distant trees

a crowd of enemies stand before him
enemies of headless suits
acting through their great desperate king
whose beard once reached the raging sea
and the sea stopped moving

how, how did it happen

suso has played on the final ladders of the mass
as he tossed a small tin can into the priest's heart

his world's now alone in the sky
alone in the lonely sky
the river's tent is broken
the last fingers of leaf
clutch and sink
into the wet bank

his agony in stony places
as an armless poet, he stands
lost in the vomiting crowd

the abstract terms of theology
were for him pregnant with meaning
transfigured by living experience
in his ardent, vivid prose
the dead bones
were once infused with life

but tonight
the light is buried
by noises and chains

but at this thin curvature of silence

he owns no wildernesses
where thought alone
can make monsters

within thy innermost
where certainly nothing else exists
where once he may have stood
in arrogance
among rook-tongued spaces

now only grit corrupts the eyes
he glowers in his sullenness
he's been maligned…
a maltreated hostage

et dimitte nobis

he perceives
all is counterfeit
all is transitory

in the labyrinth
of folding screens
his nakedness receives
the moon of punishment
and in the ashen clock
his body floats
balanced between opposites

darkness is in him
around him
everywhere it is dark
an avalanche
covers him

the oppressive weight
crushing in upon him

every meaningful mis-adventure
every empty hollowed proverb
every shallow and naked state of mind
every disconnected notion left behind
debita nostra sicut et nos

every sword that has bled my side
every scream that death begot
every notion raged in doubt
every sunless storm's shameless drought

dimittimus debitoribus nostris

every benign attempt at resolve
every scorched-savored memory
of that night

et ne nos inducas in tentationem

crying... in a mystery exposed
melody.... hiding beneath a vined fortress
a fortress protecting eternity

crying... a solemn mystery exposed
melody... yet, hiding beneath your vined fortress
gates opened...
above a night's eternity displayed

the two angels return
until now they have remained nameless
but one steps forward and says to him
my name is **armaita**…
which means 'angel of truth'

off in the distance
he saw a church…
she took him there
to the altar

she opened the bible
and lo
it was as a deep pit
into which he descended

gates opened
stretching forth
a symphony that spurns thy embrace
stretching forth
embracing, as if a midnight's requiem
so reckless… that faceless symphony

*and **armaita** proclaimed*

***suso**, walk deeply*
walk deeply… my son
lest you drown in shallowness…
the shallowness of it all

sed libera nos a malo

amen

the second angel, remained silent
and who's name, she kept secret

suso's eyes locked in on hers
and at once his eyes
were shattered in the wind

he saw no god
nor heard any
in a finite organical perception
he stretched out to the night
reached to embrace each star
until he screamed to the heavens
and they answered back...
in silence

many times, he found himself lost
in order to search for the burn
that keeps things awake
and only found the desperate
leaning over

desperate, as his thoughts give sway
as the creatures of the sky
are buried under snowlike sand

and the circle
of a strange sky
remains earthbound

for the ancient untouched statues
beseech the tender intimacy

of sleeping volcanoes

where the small clay christ
has broken its fingers
on the eternal edges

where blood flowed down the mountain
and the angels looked for it
but the chalices turned to wind
and the blood spilled from burned out stars
o' cross
o' nails
o' thorn

o' thorn nailed to bone

flowers of sketched anguish
the light buried
by noises and chains
in the obscene challenge
of rootlessness
off in the distance
there were trees grown large
trees grown numerous
where the weak were caught by the strong
all the while grinning
first coupled with…
and then devoured

plucking off first one limb
and then another
till the body was left a helpless trunk
kissing it with seeming fondness

they devoured
and savourily picked the flesh off
with a confident insolence
formed from this soil

sanctificatur nomen tuum

as if only holding a candle in sunshine
as the angels who stretched out their arms
embracing the flame of fire
until it was totally consumed

o what limb rending pains
thy fire and thy frost

thou knights of the sorrowful countenance
spinners of the spirit
glisten in all the colors of distress

pater naster, qui es in caelis

tonight… as he sleeps
under his head
there will be found
no bible
nor scrolls, egyptian, pythagorean, or platonic
but papyrus fragments
of the books of aristophanes
where strepsiades
proves that the gods do not exist
and that the weather patterns
are produced by a chorus of clouds

there will be found

not a cleave to a sympathy
be it even for higher men
into whose peculiar torture
and helplessness chance
has given him insight

and remoteness of the bird
which always flies further aloft
in order always to see more under it
and push the virtue of liberality

the abysses for the profound
for the men without solitude

suso's spirit had to develop
into subtlety and daring
from oppression and compulsion
to escape the gloomy
to an agreeable refuge
from prejudices and accidents
from men and spurious books

with foregrounds and backgrounds
to the end of which no foot may run
hidden under the mantles of light

suso… still looking into her eyes…
this angel without name

her lips moved
but in their stillness
words poured forth in the wind

we firstlings of time

with all our dangerous curiosity
our multifariousness and art of disguising
our mellow and seeming sweetness

shall we come to agreement
with our most secret and heartfelt inclinations
with our most ardent requirements

let us look for them in our labyrinths
where so many things lose themselves
so many hang behind our heads
and often enough
also, behind our understanding
but does the spirit
profit… even by this desperation
tested, put on, taken off, packed up
and studied
undergoing, enduring, interpreting
and exploiting misfortune

and whatever depth, mystery, disguise
has been bestowed upon the soul

has it not been bestowed through suffering
through the discipline of great suffering
fashioned, bruised, forged
stretched, roasted, annealed, refined

a suddenly adopted preference of ignorance
of arbitrary shutting out
a closing of windows
an inner denial

a contentment with obscurity

approval of ignorance delight
in uncertainty and ambiguity
narrowness and mystery

of the magnified, the diminished, the mishappened

the constant pressing and straining
of a creating, shaping
in its craftiness
and its variety of disguises

to bring it about
that man shall henceforth stand before man
as he is now
hardened

o' strepsiades
eternity you obliterated and erased

my hall is grief
famine is my table
hunger my knife
delay my valet
slackness my maid
precipice my gate
faintness my porch
sickness and pain my bed
and my tent is cursing and howling

render thy feeble joints
thou temper of dark

as to philosophy
by whose assistance these mysteries are developed

it is coeval with the universe itself
and however its continuity may be broken
by opposing systems
it will make its appearance
at different periods of time
as long as the sun itself
shall continue to illuminate the world

it has indeed, and may hereafter
be violently assaulted by delusive opinions
but the opposition

will be just as imbecilic
as the waves of the sea
as a temple built on a rock
which majestically pours them back
broken and vanquished
foaming to the main

III

suso entered and saw
secrets of the land unknown

the god who they created
was human work and human madness

he finds only ashes and remnants
and debris in himself
those old things have collapsed
into fantasies and imagination

as he secretly canalized
a huge river into unconscious
then simply envelops himself
in the cloak of his own imagination

as he blindfolds himself
by a self-created veil
where he becomes quite alone
with only the innermost self

her words continued
yes the nameless one… her words flowed forth…

it's okay
in writings
even before thy gospels
there was a lord
and this lord said

and wherever there is one alone

i say i am with him

so long as appearances remain appearances
they are apparent truths
but when they are accepted as real truths
at once they become
falsities and fallacies

illusions of time and space
seductions of mere outward nature
the formation of creeds and beliefs
sources of danger
where the wearied rational mind
devoid of imagination
loses its faith and energies of life

folding the pure wings of mind
seeking the places dark
abstracted from the roots of science

suso saw
the indefinite space beneath his feet
upon the verge of non-existence

the search for the bitter root
of human existence
and the globe of life blood trembling

a web dark and cold
throughout all
where the tormented element stretched
so twisted and so knotted
the meshes; twisted to the human brain
nerves changed into marrow

and the hardening of bones began

in swift diseases and torments
the woven hypocrisy
streaky slime in their heavens
brought together
by narrowing perceptions

black wind pierces the battered heart
he saw hungry beings shuffle along
toothless obscurities
who tried to smile at him

through the accursed air
these people's suffering
pierced him
entangled his soul
like barbed wire…
it gripped his heart

he went to cry out on the crossroads

he went out to weep
enveloped in mist
he touched the doors
and they wounded him

like sharp-pointed knives
then called out to the impassive faces
that were once adored like the stars
and now they showed their void

beside the cathedral
knotted to the wall

they dragged their feet
their non-descript shoes

their black stares
their tattered tins of food
from the hard sanctity of stone
its trees of tortured

adveniat regnum tuum

suso is moved…
my consciousness is frantically trying to clutch the world
the more i grasp… the more it changes
escaping through a net of abstractions

a collection of processes rather than entities
in which the whole varied world of nature
vanishes from my sight
swallowing all sounds in layer upon layer

as if a restraint of senses occurs
my mind is unable to remain in its chosen direction
and my body's in dissolution
my flesh and bones have melted together

feeling compelled to babble nonsense
my words attempt their expression
where there is an object, there no thought arises
this attempt to grasp reality has wholly ceased

it seems as if it were nothing at all
where i have so deeply immersed myself
i find myself adrift

where there is no thing, no fact, no being

today i have wiped out all the notions from my mind.
given up all desire
discarded all the words with which i thought
and entered a state of quietude... beyond all naturally
occurring forms

i have lost the boundary of my physical body
i am standing in the center of the cosmos
i see people coming towards me
but all are the same... all are me

i spoke
but my words have lost their meaning
a deception of symbols pretending to be realities
between my mind and its contents

therefore, i try and try, to imagine what i was before i
was born
but there is an absence of symmetry in the pictures
before me
a consistent avoidance of regular and geometrical
shapes
sweeping as spontaneous... rather than what i
expected

and the **second angel**, the silent one
whose words sprang forth
and who's name, she kept secret
remained by his side

suso once again look into her eyes
she takes his hand

leads him down a long stony path
that leads to water's edge

here they stayed
they watched the sunsets
the phases of the moon
the stars
the rain and the wind
and the crashing of the waves
they listen intently
as she remained still and silent

this night, they encounter a severe storm
a seismic wave crashes against the shore

suso is knocked unconscious
and dragged across the sand
the silent angel disappears

in a semi-conscious state, his thoughts carry him
to where he hears…

birds and a distant city's roar
where nobody notices the clouds
noble, but shapeless
colorless, but no less mysterious

and he proclaims…
i am standing somewhere at the edge of nerves

the scene composes, i will take it in
i am standing on a shore
the surf washes up, then uncoils as the ocean passes
over

the sand grows darker... then drains away

is this what life is supposed to be
mysteriously, i am shrinking into myself
who did you say made this place
no treachery too base to commit

all is still in my solitude of reluctance
only the sound of the sea
when did the blue fade from the rolling waves
i am staring at the face of time, watching history
disfigure the lonely

a stay against confusioned celebrations
solitary moments of consciousness ring out like a great
aria
locked in myself... plunging into seas of meaningless
like lightning stumbling and tossing into darkness

i am standing somewhere at the edge of nerves

suso witnesses what appear to be flowing wings
like a blanket covering the morning sky
and at once, the **silent angel** re-appears before him

her beauty is magnified
more enrapturing than ever
she again reaches for his hand
guiding him forward
on a long meditative walk
that night as their walk was nearing its end
she surprises him
she softly sings and tells him

tonight, i shall introduce you to god

come into the forbidding forest with me
where echoes travel
where nothing is created
and nothing is destroyed

to an uncharted path
where old landmarks disappear
and remain anchorless for a time
you press on… struggling higher

where formerly there was belief
to a place of chilling doubt
where once you were nourished
deep amidst time-honored symbols

your mind was both actor and spectator
beyond the canons of logic
and all at once
your preconceptions progressively shattered

the stories, events, incidents, and sayings
were a mixture of imagined allegories
where truths were cleverly conveyed
through the medium of symbolic myth

re-stitch together the ten-thousand pieces
where nothing becomes everything
then substitutes the heart for the stone
and thine own spirit for the scripture

where you will reach inward
behind the endless series

of disconnected thoughts
from the hand-built exterior sanctuary

to the unwrought unshaped interior stillness
where every flower is a philosopher
until the world becomes a mere shadow
here you enter a state of inner emptiness

traverse the bright inner dimensions
until the vast interconnectedness is seen
and your inner architecture
collapses altogether

and the music of the spheres merge…
see through their eyes
hear through their ears
breathe through their being

where mind is boundless
imperturbable and changeless
here, where there is no unbridgeable chasm
now listen… to the voices of silence

she disappears…

and **suso** is left all alone
in the dark

next he finds himself in the presence
of what can only be described
as something miraculous
and out of the darkness
the amphora vase is returned

peering inside, this time he sees

a series of ancient scrolls

suso reaches into the vase
and removes the scrolls
just then… a gust of wind
blows the pages out of his hands
and scatters them

onto the surface
of the glasslike sea
a circle of blue
so pale it was almost white
as the vase is smashed

into a thousand dimly sparkling pieces
smashed and infinitely old and patient
and then a ring of dark blue
so fine and sharp

no needle could have drawn it
and the sadness of time
dwelt in the blue-breathing
lost and alone and far away

deeper than the deepest well
spoke almost wholly without emphasis
and with only the subtlest coloring
as if the personal emotion

and the transition to prayer
was the moment and mark of surrender

and the words from the scrolls sparkled
against the water's reflection

as the pages lie before him across the water
he witnessed the appearance of a rainbow
amidst the evening's darkness
that re-bound the pages back together

the sun has fully set
the moonlight sparkles on the water
the night darkens the once majestic sky
the rainbow fades
the calm waters begin to rock
they crash into the night
the pages become tattered and moist
the inscriptions on each page begins to fade
the inkened inscriptions...
disappear... one by one

the ink flows from the pages
into what was calm
to a now, treacherous sea
the ink, like thick black oil
spreads from the water
to the shore
leaving a trail of death in its wake

suso dives into the sea
and attempts to retrieve the lost pages of the scroll

he sees death spreading before him...
the sea vegetation and fish
everything that is before him... perish before his eyes
he reaches for each remaining page
but as his hand grasps them
they dissolve between his fingers

soon, all the remaining pages of the scrolls perish

he swims
he strokes in every direction
he appears as a mad man
as the waves crash around him

suddenly his strength is gone
he begins to sink
the sea covers him like a cool and hardened blanket

confíteor deo omnipoténti et vobis, fratres, quia pec-
cávi nimis
cogitatióne, verbo ópere et omissióne

as he lay in darkness
he sinks into silence

i was lost beneath the cresting waves...
beneath the darkness, beneath a blackened sea
i lost my breath as i grabbed forth into the night...
the waters reflected the seven faces of a radiant moon

tightly folded and measured, let it be transformed
re-written in our prayer books and recited with beads
as we listen to ptahhotep, six-thousand guards stand
guard
protected from fear, there is no death... wrapped
securely in the armour of diomedes

all is noble
might we say
and thou hast laid it out before us
o' homer... noble one, what have you brought me

today

have you misled me with your conception
of power and lineage... be it strangely greek
but you are not so strong
nor are you particularly weak

you are neither good or bad
beautiful or ugly
favored by the gods... nor are you cursed
ah... but these words you have written, they have filled
me... they have penetrated me slowly
were they meant to enlighten
or meant to intrude
you proceeded unwelcomed, the words went down
hard
invading even my innermost thoughts, even these, you
have pursued

as a trojan warrior
heavily, i will fall in your story
i will go down... the light will fade slowly
the lands are crashing all around and inside of me

the pain of each blow, as if to my own head
i will feel each warrior's death
my senses never going numb
exultation blazes, pity is hidden, i crouch shackled
beneath even my own weakening breath

achilles... where is thy pity
has a mortal ever traveled this road
i put my lips to the hand of the man who has killed my

child
my face is hidden, if i look into your eyes my heart will
explode

oh demeter... you have summoned the gods
will they return to you thy holy child, stolen from your
arms
or receive thine acts of vengeance and famine and
death
your hymn was gentle, but the torch has gone dark, the
gods will be stripped and stand before you unadorned

kidnapped, raped and carried away
my beautiful child, my child, my darling persephone
i have hidden in wait among the mortals... i will cast
forth my spell
a blackened, hard and barren earth... cold as ice, dark
as the sea

telemachus... who is your father
have you come to know yourself
has he returned... has he lied... does he stand before
you disguised
your stale blood stain adorns the floor where he once
prayed and bowed and knelt

like a raggedly dressed stranger, bathed and anointed
with oil
your curling locks hang down like hyacinthine
i am standing at the gate of the palace
where the sweetness and misery of life are intertwined

oh, plato... tell me please, what is truth

does it exist
as if in socratic dialogue... i will dig deep
into the darkness of night, where it hangs, turns and
twists

what is truth... what is human
the ineffable rather than the known
where virtue is abandoned
and the absolute dissolves, without a scream or even a
silk-ladened moan

and you, oh dionysus... in violence you were born
to this woman, this mere mortal... you were to be her
son
fate screamed from a different text
torn apart and eaten raw... an explosion erupted, this
light was vanished and gone

until the night's lightning cracked open the sky
o' son of zeus
once torn apart, you now sit before him restored
the wild tales of the gods... divinity, ritual and rebirth

what will i now make of you, o' aeneid
read in the daylight, but never fully understood
the audacity of your scheme
legends swept into history, the prophets were
summoned

from your pen of inevitability... you have collapsed
even time and space
power and glory obediently sanctioned and divine
the empire stood, the rite broken and tarnished and

stained
in glamour, july stepped into august, as if he was truly
next in line

so defining and escapable, yet we are unaware
what gives you the right
so adverse, imposing... your actions... so abrupt
how do you grant and extinguish a life, all the while
experiencing such delight

the gods... so misbehaved
then yahweh arrived, he dismissed them all, cleansed
the alters from all that was corrupt
from mountain heights, he declared... 'you weren't
there, and you don't know'
until dionysus returned... just dropped into time,
unlike the one so abrupt

dishonor, prohibit and even tempt me
numb me, even to the pleasure i will savor
do as thou will... my desire shall be all the more
intensified
lest i dance for you and embrace my lord for my just
reward

your grace is elusive
your ways are mysterious
augustine, my friend... you stood and scoffed at such
fantasy
to punish the wicked and reward the virtuous

shall there be no struggle, no faith
how do you justify the discord, the pain, even to our

very last breath
will you sidestep even the most basic elements
our very substance, our very texture... even denying
that it all ends in death

shun the prophets, search beneath their scarlet robes
may they challenge pericles and the glory of his state
and the morality of machiavelli too
the boldness, courage... and stoically dismembered
debate

o' boccaccio, hero of lust
in, but thirteen hundred pages
our questions are answered
such dangerous words you have espoused...
threatening this ancient god and his earthly sages

eros, force of life, the builder of our cities
metaphor of energy
have you threatened the core of our understanding,
even our salvation
i have read your words of enlightenment and simplicity

are we enlightened
or have we been inflicted by a dark intellectual plague
you bragged that only you were there
but now, are you done with us... hiding deep within
your remote and secret cave

o' supreme and distant one
selling a creed to a people afraid of loneliness
to hearts that are compounded with raw elements of
the present

the skeptics turn away... standing separate and hidden
from the rest

taught by mister hume... questioning the absolute
just turn your eyes to the theater... together we weep
and sometimes we smile
our common nature speaks forth
even the villain weeps at the death of a child

they say i am lacking in my thinking
i start out orderly... only to fall into a state of utter
confusion
and watch as saint aquinas winds me up
montagne is right beside me...running through time in
his imagination

if my mind could gain clear footing
i would not write essays... i would throw away this
mantle
i would make decisions, i would stand by myself
but my mind's in apprenticeship, standing near the
galley awaiting my final trial

is there a conscience... is there really a guardian angel
does she differ from the gentle stallion, as she examines
her reflection in the mirror
i have conversed with this mighty horse, i have turned
my gaze to the stars and the clouds
and unlike my questions, pursuits and my thoughts...
found them to be so simple, so clear

to be acceding to commonplace beliefs
and undermining them at the same time

*your writing devastates us... lest we run... lest we get
out of your way
will your attempt to understanding be in vain... be
patient, read each word and stay close to the line*

*rousseau raises his pen-clasped hand; he begins to
write
tracing man, he writes with a fury
excessive idleness biting and screaming at each polar
end... no spinning axis in sight
laughing at the tears... at the cruelty... the slavery of
many*

*the ease of all that excites... the sensual and the
refined
now bent in an overindulgent pain
greedily overburdened... soul in perpetual torment
never forgetting scraps for the poor... oh the hardship
of their passion*

*bow your head and meditate, you depraved animal
you have fallen deep... you are invisible, you are
barbaric
and just like the mood of every rebellious child
presumptuously you glare back at me, as if you have
been knighted a white-gloved majestic*

*and every woman is staring back in disbelief
staring at every one of you... eyes sparkling in their
elegance
behold them... their memory and imagination in play
inspiring an inclination to harm, wearing the mask of
benevolence*

your sword is drawn, you bow is drawn too
rivalry in one hand, conflicts in the other
you are poised to strike your blow... to be trapped and
hidden, innocent child and ruthless man
never to escape this iron cage; this handcrafted and
solemn quagmire

why should a dog, a horse, a rat, have life
and thou no breath at all... is lear deluded
as flies to wanton boys, are we to gods... killing us for
sport
or is there nothing out there, are they but imagined

setting out rewards and punishments
have we risen above the point of shame
o' penelope, will you raise your lips to odysseus
will nature keep us warm, or is there really no one left
to blame

i see this man... hagel, exposed, divided and split
who's mind has become unattached, where reason
searches the shores for an alluring passion
both subject and object, both self and other
locked in a struggle, i am climbing the protruding
ropes with no end

thoughts and elements have clashed and merged
the struggle has begun
where the blind and the shapeless crystallize
the answers parade before me, dismissing each, one by
one

and so the marxian eternal cry

the hollow exhaustion at the end of the day
the scream of boredom... the dull anger and
meaningless
can you distance yourself... can you really escape

in the beginning god created the world
where there was no reason, no order, no justice
but suffering, death... where no treachery was too base
it came gift-wrapped, but was empty... mislabeled as
happiness

daylight has faded, the blue has gone from the sea
where the language shapers once stood on thy shores
whitman and nietzsche have died... nations are
desolate, withdrawn
so history exists, here comes my mistress, my soul

the next morning
the sun rises
the horizon sparkles
off in the distance

the **silent angel** re-appears
she can offer him no consolation for the loss of the
scrolls
or the desperation of his heart... or the compound
questions and tears
she stretches out her hand
to rescue **suso** from the treacherous waters
he reaches forth... but
her hand fades from his sight
and she once again disappears

in the darkness
in the crashing waves
the sharp rocks are protruding from beneath the sea

suso fights for his life
all life appears motionless before him

in the distance
even moses, abraham and david lose their stature
they stiffen
and their skin fades
as they are pelted by sharp crystals of sand

the waves cash against their weakened bodies
and they too disappear from **suso**'s sight
their image is replaced by a woman he has never seen
a woman who only goes by **"j"**

she smiles and extends her hand
suso swims toward her
she paddles away
as she paddles away
he hears her voice…

in the distance, he hears her say,

the greatest events and thoughts
the greatest thoughts
however, are the greatest events
are longest in being comprehended

the generations which are contemporary with them
do not experience such events
they live past them

something happens there

as in the realm of stars
the light of the furthest stars
is longest in reaching man
and before it has arrived
man denies that there are stars there

how many centuries
does a mind require to be understood
that there is also a standard… an etiquette therewith
such as is necessary for mind and for thy star

then she disappears from **suso**'s sight

off in the distance
he sees **armaita**
her wings are now limp and broken at her side
she stands stubbornly in the distance

waves are crashing all around her
ripping her clothes
cutting her skin
distorting her body

her blood begins to mix with a thick dark residue
that now covers the sea
the scrolls re-appear
but the words have been wiped clean
the scrolls are completely blank

what was once thick black ink-like substance
poisoning the sea
turns red

and dissipates into the depth of the water

suso is exhausted and confused
what is the meaning of all of this

suso cries out from the cold dark sea
and falls unconsciously
into the depth of the sea

only to once again awaken
having been washed onto the beach
carried by the waves

he lays broken, naked and bleeding
the morning is dark
it is cold
he is totally alone

*misereátur nostri omnípotens deus et
dimíssis peccátis no- stris*

my limbs are failing
and my mouth is parched
my body trembles
my hair stands on end
the sacred bow gandiva
slips away from my grip
and my skin is on fire

a total deprivation
without any support
or hope for its return

oscillations of consciousness
swinging between two worlds

as a helpless prey
pushed into a new world
where it does not feel at home
darkness and confusion
where the old and known supports are withdrawn

consciousness overstretched
broken up
tossed back to an old and lower level

all contact vanishes
all that matters
seems dead

grief increases with sorrow
giving vent to loud cries
which cannot be stifled
not a pain that is felt in the body

but in the depths of the soul
a dark rapture
where the pulse is feeble
as if at the point of death

and the natural heat of the body fails
suspended in mid-air
can neither touch the earth
or mount to heaven
burning with consuming thirst
but cannot reach the water

suso now dwells in a darkness
which seems to hold no promise of a dawn

have the scroll been taken from him
was the world not yet ready
for these words to be revealed

the more clear the light
the more does it blind the eyes of the owl
and the more he tries to look at the sun
the feebler grows his site

and the more his weak eyes are darkened
thou are like a hare hiding in a bush
who is frightened by the whispering leaves
thou are also frightened

every day by the griefs
that that come to thee
thou dost turn pale at the sight
of those who speak against thee

it pained him that he did not know
where the universe ended
he stared for some appreciable time
before transferring his rapt attention to the sky

and while in that vast solitude
to which the tide of things had borne him
he appeared to breathe
and live but for himself alone

o' genius of the heart
great mysterious one
you… the tempter-god and born rat-catcher
of thy consciences

whose voice can descend
into the nether-world of every soul
who neither speaks a word
nor casts a glance

o' genius of the heart
you impose silence and attention
on everything loud and self-conceited
on the souls of the smooth
as well as the rough

and make them taste a new longing
to lie placid as a mirror
that the deep heavens
may be reflected in them

o' genius of the heart
and thy hasty hand
as you hesitate in your grasp
with scents of hidden and forgotten treasure

a drop of goodness
under thick dark ice
a divining-rod
for every grain of gold
long buried and imprisoned
in mud and sand

o' genius of the heart
never favored or surprised
never gratified and oppressed
or newer than before

broken up

blown upon
and sounded
by a thawing wind

more uncertain
more fragile, more bruised
but full of hopes
which as yet lack names

suso collapses
a man betrayed
suffering permanent, obscure and dark
as if sharing the nature of infinity

beyond that divide
he screams 'hypocrisy'
his soul squints

alone
amid the heart of many thousand mists
that came to him
and left him on the heights

among the rocks
he will go
and still look up to the sun and clouds
and listen to the wind

and, as before
hear the howling shadows
and the windows weave over
with curses of iron

in unseen conflicts with shapes

this self-contemplating shadow
obscured with mourning
his bosom earthquaked with sighs

lying on the verge of the deep
as thy dark clouds ascend
thy black forests and floods
a horrible waste to his eyes

travelling outside of humanity
beyond the stars in chaos
in caverns
of the mundane shell

looking into the black water
mingled with tears
weeping into the atlantic deep
yet still in dismal dreams

like the black storm
coming out of chaos
where human thought is crushed
beneath the iron hand

I V

suso now strives to rise
to walk into the deep
but strength failing
forbade and down
with dreadful groans
he sinks down

wandered away
into the chaotic void
lamenting with thy shadow
o dweller of outward chambers
vaporous shadow in a void

is the world not yet ready
for these words to be revealed

are their hearts
shut up in integuments
of frozen silence

have waves of pearl
became a boundless ocean
bottomless

off-grey obscurity
filled with clouds and rocks
and whirling waters
ascending and descending
in the horrid void
silent, calm, motionless

ah… but for **suso**

he sees a whale in the sea
and it's drinking his soul away
o' what limb rending pains he feels

thy fire and thy frost
ashamed of his own song
enraged he swung

to generations that in future times forget
as the morning comes
as the night decays
what god is he
that writes laws of peace
and clothes himself in a tempest

what pitying angel
lusts for tears
and fans herself with sighs

what crawling villain
preaches abstinence
and wraps himself in the fat of lambs

devouring and being devoured

dóminus sit in corde tuo et in lábiis tuis, ut digne
et competénter annúnties evangélium suum

suso will roam

on dark and desolate mountains
in troubled mists over-clouded
by the terrors of struggling times

in thoughts perturbed
they rise from the bright ruins
of silence following

obscure, enclosed
the stone of night
the amphora vase...

the words inscribed
the secrets inside
times on times

he will divide
measuring space by space
in his ninefold darkness

they began to weave
the curtains of darkness
those shrunken eyes

clouded over
discerned not
their woven hypocrisy
brought together
by narrowing perceptions
just as moses beheld

upon the mount
forms of dark delusion
as the thunder-stone was molded

amidst a globe of wrath
roaring with fury
and even this day

the tree still grows
over the void enrooting itself
all around an endless labyrinth of woe

at once **amraita** appeared before him and
proclaimed...

curious dreamer, gentle wanderer
let us talk of matters
about the god you have never met
and the meaning of this mystery

you will escape... deep into the jungle
remote from the haunts of men
where maybe you will find
the knowledge of nature's laws, complete

you will cross the sacred precincts
and stand at the threshold
midway along the mystical path
to the sanctuary of mysteries

into solitary places
and wander into a shadowy vagueness...
in that concentration of stillness
into a place deeper than thought

to you, o' **suso**
the gates shall open

stretching forth
embracing, as if a midnight's requiem
so reckless... that faceless symphony

walk deeply... my son

walk deeply...
walk deeply... my son
lest you drown in shallowness...

the shallowness of it all

sed libera nos a malo
amen

walk deeply, he must...
soft and bent are the bones of man
see thy salt tears

as they flow down
the steps of their empty house
noxious clouds hovering thick

over the disorganized mortals
till petrific pain
scurfed over the lakes
as the bones of man... solid and dark
the eyes of man
a narrow orb
closed up and dark

*o' **suso***
can such an eye judge of the stars
and looking through
measure the sunny rays

can such an ear
filled with the vapors of the yawning pit
pretend to judge
the pure melodious harp struck by a hand divine

can such closed nostrils
feel a joy
or tell of autumn fruits
when grapes and figs
burst their covering to the joyful

of labyrinthine intricacy
twenty-seven folds of opaqueness
as the sculptor silent
stands before his forming image

while you o' **suso**
a mortal toy
sit frozen in the rock of horeb

pater naster, qui es in caelis

seek not thy hidden mysteries
beyond the skies
where chaos dwells
and ancient night

sanctificatur nomen tuum

where you shall no longer dare
to mock with the aspersion of madness
you who sits in contemplation
silently plotting questions
like a thief in a cave

in your vase
think not of what may be
as if, there you will find
milton's shadow

as a dove upon the stormy sea

dear wanderer, who are you
but full of hopes
full of new wills and currents
seeking the solitude of the fields

ah… but there are theories
left unexplained
of the world… of the soul
the finite and the infinite

a rendezvous of questions
meanings… scribbled in a big book
pages filled with black letters
where every opinion is a hiding place

where every word is a mask…
in a world of dreams
where the secrets we are anxious to possess
are guarded by sages

oh, dear wanderer
let the poisoned arrow be removed
where in the stronger winds
two parallel lines will surely meet

take breathtaking leaps
where metaphor is everything
where even the lie
shall show us truth

where the word
though ever invisible and unattainable

indistinct and formidable
gallops into the corridors of the labyrinth

perhaps nothing at all exists
so, hang by your jaws
on the skirts of the clouds
beyond empty... beyond the non-void

V

the **silent angel** appears before him
she further admonishes

suso...display thy giant form
awake o' sleeper of the land of shadows

reach out to the ancients
let their motifs
crash in upon your soul
absorb their meaning
you, the enlightened one
let heaven be young

awaken
to sites and sounds
of abstract philosophy
warring in enmity against imagination

proclaim to the sky
thy holy wrath's deep deceit
cannot avail against you

let your eyes open
to awkwardness armed in steel
folly in a helmet of gold
weakness with horns and talons
ignorance with a ravening beak

waiting for some break in ritual
to strike
the authentic sea

against this onslaught
these casual blasts of ice
that wrestle at his questions
like seven wild beasts

as if a chilly god stands before you
a god of shades
with words, like locusts
drummed in the darkening air

perplexed, **suso** wonders
is this an answer
or merely a repetition of the question

thrusting himself forward
into an ever-deepening sea
and a new distrust

it is now, me alone
the one to devise cause, sequence, reciprocity
relativity, constraint, number, law
freedom, motive and purpose

and me alone, who is to interpret and intermix
this symbol-world
as being-in-itself, with things

am i to conclude that man's darkness
sits in between the night and day
an act that once more
shines amidst the depth of the sacred, the mysterious
and the myth

the **silent angel** continues…

dante saw deity
as a flame or river of fire
that filled the universe...
and caught to his heart
for one brief moment
his mind smitten
by the blinding flash of the uncreated light

at that moment
he knew that he had resolved reality's last paradox

not so ignatius
as he left manresa
solitarily, maimed, ignorant and poor

he whose task and practice it is
to investigate souls
will avail himself
of many varieties of this very art
to determine the ultimate value of a soul
the unalterable, innate order of rank
to which it belongs
he will test it by its instinct
for reverence, difference...
difference engendering hate

but **suso...** when any holy vessel
any jewel from closed shrines
any book bearing the marks of great destiny
is brought before you

there is an involuntary silence
a hesitation of the eye

a cessation of all gestures
by which it is indicated that a soul feels
the nearness of what is worthiest of respect

books of such profoundness
and supreme significance
require for their protection
an external tyranny of authority
in order to acquire the period of thousands of years
which is necessary to exhaust and unriddle them

nothing is perhaps so repulsive
as their lack of shame
the easy insolence of eye and hand
with which they touch and taste

and it is possible
to be deceived
with regard to origin
with regard to their lowly status
in appearance… in body and soul

don't be deceived…

in the writings of a recluse
one always hears something
of the echo of the wilderness
something of the murmuring tones

and timid vigilance of solitude
in his strongest words
even in his cry itself
there sounds a new and more dangerous kind of
silence

of concealment

you have at last to play your last card
as protectors of truth upon earth
as though the truth
were such an innocent and incompetent creature
as to require protectors
against involuntary vulgarizations
against falsifications

against ill-smelling books
where the odor of paltry people clings to them
and even where they reverence

and if
with the virtuous enthusiasm
and error
one may wish to do away altogether
with the seeming world
nothing of your truth would thereby remain

suso at once asks…

have the texts of the scroll
disappeared under their interpretation
was there truth
hidden inside the amphora vase…
words of handpicked verses

queens of the night
verses from divine
a truth injurious and dangerous
such that one succumbed by a full knowledge of it
could not endure

which required that it be
veiled, sweetened, damped
and falsified

that neither the courageous
nor honorable could read
the content of the scrolls

until made ludicrously superficial
as green-meadow happiness of a herd
with unhesitating fingers for the intangible
with teeth and stomachs for the most indigestible

is it here
that we may become
the born
the sworn
the jealous friends
of our own profoundest midnight
and midday solitude

the most daring of all interpreters
to exhibit these words
in endless and impossible modifications
in all their own disguises and multiplicities
as a miracle of the inversion of valuations

as if they heard some evil-threatening sound
in the distance

if it is so
what then do we know of ourselves…

a suddenly adopted preference of ignorance

an inner denial
a contentment with obscurity
with the shutting-in horizon

an acceptance and approval of ignorance
delight in uncertainty and ambiguity
an exulting enjoyment of arbitrary
out-of-the-way narrowness and mystery
of the magnified
the diminished and the misshapened

the **silent angel** responds

but at the bottom of our souls
there is certainly something unteachable
a granite of spiritual fate
with passages and galleries
where there are caves
hiding-places
and dungeons therein

where the charm of the mysterious
is acquainted with the bypaths to chaos

ah, but man doth loves the clouds
and all that is obscure
everything uncertain and growing
in the deep
in nothing but darkness

go… send out for the thunder
a thunder of colors from the four directions
where clouds drape the evening sun

where the mighty visions are shattered
one and all...
on the rocks that ring the world
in that silence, where we are between two thoughts

there, we create ourselves within time
compassionately arising
we are all that bodhisattva
simultaneously bound and free

come... arouse your fascination
listen to the music of the spheres
mystical sounds reverberating
the discernment of the real, the unreal, the illusory

behold the movement of the rock
with patterns of energy in constant motion
of what you believe to be inanimate
the states of vibration... the mantra-shastra

to the experience, not of the unknown
but of the absolutely unknowable
an evocation of your senses
breaking all contact with meaning

as if on an abstract level
where the influx of thoughts flow into your mind
here, break down the walls of the ego
to a wind-still condition... where thoughts arise then
disappear

seek the distortion-less manifestation
recover the ever-present...
where you will find signposts of rajas

shaping forms of existence

disentangle the webs of your imprisoned mind
destroy delusions and illusions
soften and tame the roving senses
silently traverse their inner dimensions
there is movement…
in this mind-transcending consciousness
a vast expression of interconnectedness
… of being-ness

embrace the mandala, dismiss the fallible
exercise the gnostic understanding
become unshackled to the mystery…
enveloped in the uninterpreted

let the branches grow downward
and their roots ascend skyward
alter the cosmos,
overcome your scattered state

stand fiercely…
drink the nectar from a simpler rose
connect to the impulse beyond the self
let sattva reflect your 'being'

is there a visible material realm
or rather, a startlingly revealed illusion…
a dimension of nature's pulsating vibrance
hidden beyond the canons of logic, theory and dogma

where reality stands naked…
and all at once our preconceptions are shattered
where rajas and tamas shape all forms

and the self has become silent and still

suso responds…

but the sacred words
as they are reverenced
are they not, but mere fiction
composed afterwards
in the world of historical values
spurious coinage
poured out to the hands of intoxicated adulators
disguised in their creations…
unrecognizable from their original intent

suso, once again moves to the water
he lets the waves cash against his weakened body
and the woman
who goes by '**j**' re-appears
she, again extends her hand

as she speaks

the greatest events and thoughts
are longest in being comprehended

as in the realm of stars
the light of the furthest stars
is longest in reaching man
and before it has arrived
man denies that there are even stars

how many centuries
does a mind require to be understood

i… an unknown author

have composed a work
that has formed the spiritual consciousness
of much of the world

the original author of what is now
attributed to prophets
yet... my words have been
censored, revised and distorted
across twenty centuries

you see the meaningless
the mysteries and the miseries
you see everything in a thousand forms
i am just a poet
with a desire to befriend the flowers and the storm

man, a stranger to himself
has found more void than fullness
resisting imagination, persisting in his soul
my scrolls once laid before them
they were blessed and unrolled

their prayers and an empty sky
but don't laugh at the virgin
the signs are obscure, don't be confused
acquiesce to the myth... the profound and the truth
where matter and spirit shall meet and marry...
i will walk before you in a ten-fold disguise
cut these words and watch them bleed
measure every angle of the morning skies

suso now turns to **amraita**
who now stands at his side...

and asks… who is she
who is **j**

amraita turns toward **j**
with outstretched wings
that beat over the sand and the waves…
and she speaks

oh, mother of solomon
writer of words
words … censored, distorted and revised
by ancient priests and cultic scribes

speak to us
we have come to sit beneath your tree
we demand the truth
listening …
we can only imagine what you really mean

we followed you to kenoma
to cosmological emptiness
where we wandered and wept
where the characters are interpreted
and meaning is suppressed

i hardly know who you are or what you mean
you once walked the old hills of judea
a gentle god by your side
but now, only the squirrels are looking back at you

we stood beneath the last starless night
in empty halls … on vacant seats
in this place, a once hallowed sanctuary
with no presence … heaven left empty

but we have finally met ourselves
we are quiet and now stand alone
o' mother of solomon
you have unmasked the world
you stand in eternal silence...
will your eyes ever be unveiled

suso stares at nothing in particular
wondering if his dreams have not as yet ended

he heard the words
words changing color

where radically altered men
step in the required direction
of infallibility
a paradigm and paragon
metamorphoses as vapor, mist, cloud
rain, sleet, snow and hail

forms in loughs and bays and gulfs
and bights and guts and lagoons
sounds and fjords and minches
and tidal estuaries and arms of sea

its solidity in glaciers, icebergs, icefloes
its docility in millwheels, turbines, dynamos
in navigable, floating and graving docks
derivable from harnessed tides

shaking foundations
the candles dimmed, and the church remained
standing tall
shaken by condemnation

your papers, your books laid out before me, you nearly
decided to burn them all

your vainglorious communiqué
why did you hide them, even from me
yes, your writings inflamed, excited and blasphemed
re-written and dried, they were rescued from the
bottom of the sea

the sun slowly set, the church bells rang
at d'alibert's home just off the seine
dukes, lawyers, mathematicians
clergymen, aristocrats and friends

in a vault of honor, at rest with the holiness of st.
genevieve
all the saints bones… quietly crumbled into ruin
placed in a garden
alongside the gods and their statues and their tombs

o' illustrious and learned one
you left us your thoughts… radical enlightenment in
stone
from salt crystals to god's grace, from human emotion
to jupiter's moons
all the while you were staring down as if from your
pantheon throne

but the god's fought back… filling their cathedrals with
miles of empty space
columns standing like trees in a desert of marble
beauty alternating with violence
elegantly littered, a sonorous cascade of sculpted and

chiseled rubble

the stately flow of a falsely labeled past
jumbled by a deforming present
the lights of holiness flickered and dimmed
a world stage ready to fade, in spite of our noblest
sentiment

your life… so packed into the years
a mind reaching out to a world that secretly revolved
the seeds will rise and become spring's flowering trees
will you ever be understood, will this puzzle ever be
solved

suso… now talking to himself
overhears his own words
as he ponders

i will not go mad
nor allow a hole to pierce me
in the threshold of my consciousness
let not this adventure miscarry

on this quest
this hero's fight
i feel alone
i have no weapons…

let me cross over these dark waters
and arrive safely
on the other side

suso imagines madness
as he imagines a poem

a prophecy
a third testament
in no way subservient to the old or the new
the koran or the torah

imagines the writings
of the scrolls
and the cracked and broken vase

he will find the words
read until they bleed
until the words destroy the distinction
between sacred and secular
of prophecy and poem

the shorter my possession of life
the deeper and fuller i must make it
and o' the tragedy
of a god who hides himself

i shall become the shepherd
who has learned the meaning of all winds
of blasts of every tone

a new language
of symbol and myth
of knowledge
preserved and bequeathed

from age to age
modified by genius
but never abandoned
borrowed peacefully

the forms which appear in matter
shadows falling upon shadow
imitations of being
flowing about a formless semblance

suso secretly canalizes a huge river
into his unconscious
then simply envelops himself
in the cloak of his own imagination
as he blindfolds himself
by a self-created veil

thy ten overcomings
thy ten reconciliations
and the ten truths and the ten laughters
cradled by forty thoughts

where the archetypes
are caught in symbols
not as fantasies
of a solitary dreamer

suso wonders aloud
is the sea of time and space
located in the empty heart

this land of woven labyrinths...
the voids and land of clouds
a lake not of water, but of space

of poetic symbols
blind forces that step out onto the stage
or who merely haunt it
mysteriously embodying the character

the hard task of understanding metaphor
and to catch, at the speed of the voice
the rhythmic design of the motif

plots and counterplots
tensions and counter-tensions

will the scrolls re-appear
the words
which have been wiped clean...
left completely blank
as if flared up and burned
and turned into crumbled ash

questions of the mind
rules surrounded by emptiness, neatly spaced
the answers are deeply hidden
mental powers whose origins can't be traced

stepping inward... penetrating from outside this realm
i am lying here uncomfortably
where patterns of our existence sit transient
and here i will find... this unexplained mystery

chaotic and dynamic
elaborately constructed
forms are changing before me
thoughts turned upside down... i sit confused

beyond even the conception of the colors
beyond what's been conceivably measured...
let me embrace free will
let me embrace the pain and the melody

my thoughts are now patterns, before me they deepen
some are complex, some extraordinarily plain
this is the edge of chaos
the path that leads to all that is unknown

thoughts processing in the purest form
as if inhabiting a world of their own
eluding computation
elaborately constructed, the breath of life is blown

is there something in the stars
a universe that obeys
why should we be forbidden
or shall i be... unsettled and betrayed

different from all the pictures
a process of deception
physically entangled... a universe unexplained
separated by a moment, lying beyond all computations

making known the quantum choices
the 'external mind'
the deep, the shallow, the rough and entangled
the machine sits so unpolished... yet so refined

the arrogance of our age
to believe that we now know...
then nature smiles
in an unsympathetic wave, she ends this show

suso continues his search
for these ashes
scattered on the ground
that he may

unwind time
and bring them together again
retake the form
they had before
when at first it appeared…
will it be possible to decipher

just then…
the **silent angel** and **"j"** appear before **suso**
but they are indistinguishable
they have become one before his eyes
and their voice spoke forth

suso… come
tonight, i shall introduce you to god

suso asks
are you the virgin
who is wading on the strand

just then
in her voice
lines of understanding emerge
yet appear countered
by images and thoughts
going in the opposite direction

dim effigies rumble past
and quickly disappear into foggy horizons
only to be replaced by other images
these interlocking allusions
a prodigious, multifaced monomyth

like desolate mountains
rifted furious
by the black winds of perturbation

mountains all around
hanging frowning cliffs
and all between
an ocean of voidness unfathomable

a void between fire and fire

in a language of simile, metaphor and allegory
of interweaving historical facts

a word painting
of the tumultuous inner battles

suso now asks
who are you **j**

she then spoke these words
in a soft voice of angelic sound

i was sent forth
from the power
and i have come to those
who reflect upon me
and i have been found
among those who seek after me

look upon me
you who reflect upon me
and you hearers, hear me

you who are waiting for me
take me to yourselves
and do not banish me
from your sight

thoughts and feelings
memories and perceptions
the vibrations of energy
flowing within a field of awareness

where truth is but one path
dressed in different costumes

do not make your voice hate me
nor your hearing

do not be ignorant of me
anywhere or any time

i am the honored one
and the scorned one
i am the whore
and the holy one

i am the wife
and the virgin
i am the mother
and the daughter

i am the silence
that is incomprehensible
and the idea
whose remembrance
is frequent

why, you who hate me
do you love me
and hate those
who love me

you who deny me
confess me
and you who confess me
deny me

for i am knowledge
and ignorance
i am shame
and boldness

you will find me in the kingdoms

i, i am godless
and i am the one whose god is great

i am unlearned
and they learn from me

so, take me to yourselves
from places that are ugly and in ruin
and rob from those which are good
even though in ugliness

i am peace
and war has come because of me

hear me, you hearers
and learn of my words
you who know me
i am the hearing
that is attainable to everything

i am the speech
that cannot be grasped
i am the name of the sound
and the sound of the name

i am the sign of the letter

look then at my words
and all the writings
which have been completed
my thoughts arise out of nowhere
and dissolve into nothing
into stillness

boundaries are fluid and ever shifting

i am the sound of the bird
as i am the one hearing the bird

on the canvas which is me
i unfold the universe
let it flow into form
and coalesce into patterns of embodiment

a vastness filled with quiet presence
and in that vastness, little by little
something indescribable starts to be revealed

my thoughts, feelings, and perceptions
arise and dissolve within awareness

o' muses
o' genius of art
o' memory whose merit
has inscribed inwardly those things i saw
help me fulfill the perfection of your nature

and then she said to **suso**…

take my measure now
appraise my powers before you trust me
to venture through that deep passage
where i would be your guide

i was never created…
that my life begins
is but a masterful delusion
i was the cosmos, a solitary circle

wrenched away from the universe
a piece of life
deliberately broken off
i have become the rocks and trees

the clouds and waters
an intelligible form
of the geometer and architect
a mathematical crystal composed

i will always be living
among blue mountains and green trees
whether straight or curved, jagged or gnarled
the very texture of this line is full of life and verve

a form slightly eccentric and at times out of shape
with splashes and gaps of a roughly stroked brush
interpreting the world by grasping it, piece by piece

and yes, my friend...
you too are the cosmos, the living circle

then she was silent

suso
overcome by his soul
on that dark slope
now voided the undertaking
that he had so quickly embraced

you, the blessed qualified one
you, who understands, interprets and evaluates
emerged deeply from the milky ocean...
rise now into your magical trance

emerge from the darkened abyss of unconsciousness

a steady river of quietness flows near me
penetrating the inner reaches of my being
the chains of my mind are broken
leading me into solitary places... to the sanctuary of
mysteries

where i let my thinking stop
in a place deeper than thought
in an ocean of blazing light
outside even the rim of world consciousness

i will retire into this solitary place
into the darkness of a mountain tunnel
then turning it backwards
let me be carried into the light again

having gone through dark nights of the soul
receded into shadowy nothingness
where my own existence
seemed, but a small fragment of the universe

o' j... is the garden paradise
still somewhere to be found
or is it hidden... is it shut off
by mountains or seas
or the torrid regions which cannot be crossed

has it been transformed above the summit
of the peaks of mount meru
in the middle of an imagined ocean
at the level of prakriti
where no algebraic root can be found

was there ever was a time
when time was not
when this kaleidoscopic play
of eternity would have ceased

when light and darkness' danced
and the cosmic shadow play
stood at once, beyond and within
in a rapture... in the void of eternity

or, is there everywhere in a mystic awe
a continuous ripple of transformation
an unfolded, unfolding as if in a symphonic theme
announced, amplified in this... a slow and majestic flow

j then says to **suso**

is it from that encompassing state
you long to see again

o' **suso**... you yearn for the answer... deeply

so i will show you
trusting your eloquence
whose gift brings honor
both to yourself
and to all those who listen

having said this
she turned toward him... face-to-face
the splendor of her eyes lucent with tears

as flowers bend

and are shrunken by night
then at dawn
unfold and straighten on their stems
to wake brightened by sunlight

you too shall break free from all cages
and give way
to something rich
to something silent and still

plunge into the intense
the unraveling cascade of life
collapsing and disintegrating
into a pathless land

i am snapped...
of the dull and familiar
where they unfold... and vanish in an instant
here i will confront the wonder

so, this night i will take you to...
to the scrolls that disappeared
in the darkening air

so **suso** grew strong again
her words restored his spirit
for he feels eager to go
and cleave to his first intention

two will share one will
together, she his teacher, master, and his guide
and when she moved, he followed after
and entered on that deep and savage road

so, he spoke

strange soul of the space in my veins
where the dancing rains wander untouched
last curves of air, and on mounds of saffron

crowned with a helmet and dark hair
almost nameless
i only know you by "j"
in the dark air
silent... you stand as night

you... the guardian of the secret codes
forsook the ancient mansion
your soft hands draw the indelible line
and every minute has an azure tent with silken veils
and every hour
has a bright golden gate
carved with skill

stretching
from zenith to nadir
in midst of chaos
heights magnificent weave overtrembling
to euphrates and hindu

j responds

i will take you
to the nile and back
in clouds
osiris, isis, orus
in despair, they will sleep on the stone

with intellectual spears
and long winged arrows of thought
infected with the error and illusion

let us enter them
in dreams of soft deluding slumber

they looked up
and saw the prince of light
with splendor-faded-self-delusion
a watery vision

just then… as if as a crack of lightning
j trembled
and covered her face
if thou withdraw thy breath
behold i am oblivion
she ceased…
the shadowy voice was silent
but the cloud hovered over their heads
suso beheld her with wonder
with commanding speed
she took a moment of time
drawing it out
with many tears and afflictions

the tremblings
vibrated through the limbs

she now stood
turning the iron spindle of destruction
from heaven to earth
invisible to **suso**

but not invisible to her

the sun shrank
even the heavens have shrunk away
into the far remote
and the trees and mountains withered
into indefinite cloudy shadows
in darkness and separation
by invisible hatreds adjoined
they seem so remote
so separate

rigid skies sloping
where the colonies of planets
devour pieces of sky

then **j** spoke…
the masters
have read volumes
and turned over the leaves

with only a plastic expression
staring back silently
sometimes forgotten
an echo of a passing century

a panic and then a conquest
of the star strewn darkness
of wonders of a tainted world…
and the sunrise stares back in indifference

and the slumber of the gods
what have their cathedrals become
if not of a world of voided dreams

subordinated words and hollowed museums

holy communion...
and we stare into the statue's face
the painter to a painting he once saw
a language long ago modified
where myths and legends embrace, turn and withdraw

and amphitrite merges into the open sea
this is not a sacrament... this is not a dream

turn away from me, don't look back... just run
for even death will not still my voice
though forsaken... never shall i be bowed and broken
in my revolt against fate, i'll not stand devoid of choice

my poetry is haunted by a voice
with words that scream to harmonize
this stairway, i have built step by step
through underlying currents and rising tides

where three crosses are etched in solitude
where shepherds are gathered round a child
where apollo's face is transformed
and venus becomes the mistress of the world

you must bring your own lamp
don't paint the shadows
paint night itself, a darkness devoid of sound
confronting the sea of time, where you know you must go

that's where serenity dwells
in an eternal stillness
where no neutral form exists

where there is neither deliberate nor consciousness

in a vastness of unmoving forms
of sleeping armies of long ago
one-thousand years have piled above the dust
your face is staring back, with a reflection you don't
even know

follow each movement of my trembling hand
filter what you see
what i paint is my inner voice
value disintegrated into plurality

the cult of reason
a carnival of madmen
the iron hand of destiny
venus envelops all in a caress that knows no end

through walls and halls
where eternity withdrew
before nights of attraction and isolated imaginings
my voice arises from a pregnant solitude

lost in my soul
as if, in an idle dream
shifting the voice of destiny
passionately, i will condemn this unholy scheme

it is well
but i will teach you
to read the living book
wherein everything lives

saint thomas aquinas once declared

that there was somewhere on earth…
a garden of paradise

a paradise shut off
from the habitable world
by mountains or seas
or by some torrid region
which cannot be crossed

take my hand
and we will cross
the mountains and seas
i will take you there

where illusions have been dispelled
i will tell you the thoughts of man
that have been hid from of old
where every human heart
has gates of brass
and bars of adamant
which few dare unbar
because of dread

awake
i hear thy confllictions
sing in the sky
and round my limbs

of gold and jewels
a sublime ornament
a couch of repose
with sixteen pillars

canopied with emblems

and written verse
verse, ordered
and measured

from whence, time shall reveal
within the human heart
whose gates are closed
with solemn sound

from the inner sanctuary
what is above is within
and earth
and all you behold

though it appears without
it is within your imagination
of which this world in linear form
is but a shadow

i melt my soul in reasonings
among the towers of heshbon...
and mount zion
a cruel rock

no dew nor rain
a coldness
no more will the spring of the rock appear
their pillars lay in ruins

they are become narrow places
in a little and dark land
where their tents are fallen
their children dashed

where gods finger
wrote the law... then wept
i wrote the law
and i smiled

how could anything originate
out of its opposite
truth out of error

how much vulnerability
does this masquerade
of that sickly recluse betray
from the domain of dangerous knowledge
giving our senses
a passport to the superficial

i shall teach you
that as long as thou feel the stars as above thee
thou shall not lack the eye of the discerning one

thou hath been
a man made out of words
and there is an ultimate changelessness in each of us
a fixed position that we must occupy

if prophecy be madness
as they lie hid
in all external forms...
caverns' there were
within your mind
which sun could never penetrate
my work was buried deep
in the world's mind

now is the time to re-write those words
where i am from
one has taught me the song
the other... silence

wherever this word is to be heard
it must occur in stillness and in silence
there we can hear it
and understand it

in that state of unknowing
where we know nothing
it becomes apparent and is revealed

unknowing precedes the knowing
in knowledge and dogmas
there is danger

j takes his hand
i will take you there...

we shall break away from the anguish
of being thus thrown like a wisp of straw
into this maelstrom of worlds
into an absurd universe
devoid of meaning
in which you feel as if you are nothing

and we will walk
on the vaults of the sky
and on the sands of the deep

j holds a rock in her hand
and says:

when i touch a rock
i never touch it as inanimate
the tree too is spirit... mind

the rock is spirit, mind
the air, the stars, the moon
are object of our consciousness

we shall lower ourselves into this
let ourselves downward
hand over hand
as on a rope that quivers
over the unsearched

we shall do this
conceived of each other
in a darkness
a darkness which you will remember

in rituals, etiquette
the blurring of terms
silence
not absence of words or music
or even raw sounds

are the words of the prophets and disciples
the theologians and scholars
the monks
and the priest and the scribes...
are their words true

revelation always goes beyond the literal
and the literal
surely leads one

to misunderstand the revelation

suso asks **j**

will you lead me in
the journey downward
into the dark
into the shadows
and upon return, to attempt to name it

j says yes

… but the shadow is a tight passage
a narrow door
whose painful construction no one is spared
who goes down to the deep well

for what comes after the door is
a boundless expanse
full of uncertainty
with no inside and no outside

no above and no below
no here and no there
no mine and no thine
no good and no bad

it is the world of water
where all life floats in suspension

from a low hill in the athi plains
where i once watched the vast herds of the wild
grazing in soundlessness… stillness
from time immemorial

touched only by the breath of a primeval world

i felt then as if i were the first woman
the first creature to know that all this is...
that the entire world round me
is still in its primeval state
though, it did not know that it was
and then, in that one moment
the world sprang into being

... without that moment it would never have been

and then i began to write
my story... a beautiful story

later men called it
the book of genesis

ah **suso**...
we are both
and we are nothing and something
we are tiny and dependent
we are in touch
with the macrocosm of the universe

here the bridge
from dogma to inner experience
has broken down

once determined by formal notions
symmetry with supreme lucidity

we reduce everything to atoms
then we come to electrons and protons
we are always trying to find what is behind it all

what is it… all woven in

at last, one comes to something
which cannot be named
cannot be seen
the hidden mystery
on which everything is woven
the world of the gods
the world of the sky and of the earth
are all woven… pervading all

penetrated to the depths of the psyche
and discovering its original ground

the hymns of the rig veda
the poems of homer
the bible…
as much poetry as prose
and its earliest strata are all poetic
is the expression of the whole man
it expresses not merely his mind
but his sensations
his feelings
his heart's affections

we have broken
the link between mind and heart
intellect and sense
thought and feeling

the world of the imagination
the world of integral wholeness
the world of myth

we need to return
to those deep places
where the world speaks through us once again

with the loss of them
there follows uncertainty
and with uncertainty, disequilibrium

the ultimate divine mystery is sought
beyond all human categories of thought and feeling
beyond names and forms
beyond any concept of mercy or wrath
beyond the chooser of one people
comforter of those who pray
and destroyer of those who do not

o' **j**
what will become of us
if we desert the foundations of our own culture
as though they were errors outlived
like homeless pirates
settled with thievish intent on foreign shores

my dear **suso**

unwarp thy mind
from thy intellectual habit
biased by what it already knows

until there are no axioms
no more dogmas
until there is only wonder

i will take you

to the heights of herat
to the mountain of kaf
beyond the limits of the avicenna
there you will look into your own heart

where the ground
is a still stillness
with no motion in itself
and where sparks burst into flashes

up high and down below
then quiet down
and then rise back up high
beyond, beyond

o' **suso...**
you have slept for a million years
let not rational doctrine
obscure the mystical vision
this is the tendency of the rational mind
to seek to dominate the truth

let me take you to the edge
to the edge of consciousness
the edge of chaos and order
the edge where creativity happens
to the edge of understanding

you are as old as homer
as modern as sartre or kant
not unlike the stargazers of the temples...
where nearby, the philosophers grimly claw at the sand

question everything

infect the inquisitor with perplexity
with complete and breathtaking abandonment
let the luminous essence remain elusive

contemplate and scrutinize
the riddle of the sphinx
meander with intent
and glare unmoved as a transient visitor

step fully into your own consciousness
to the depth of a pure 'isness'
utterly innocent... until
clouds of knowledge have disappeared

where 'i' is just a linguistic convenience
because inside there is no longer an entity
as your 'self' arises from timeless depths
transcending the foreign, the cold and the many-sided

be aroused with myths and marvels
walk slowly through the magic of time
as everything is sanctified
let the vanished gods to you re-appear

with a contented mind and placid countenance
climb the heights of mandara
stand in awe before their outstretched peaks
behold... they uphold the corners of the sky

lay prostrate in the mosque, the church, the temple
kneel before the alter
sit with folded legs in the ashram of silence
take refuge and bow in hollowed grounds

as the doubter, become the doubt
and out of persistent wonder and fear
in the undwelling of obscure souls
in the presence of hermit saints... read the forest-texts

stand between knowledge and ignorance
where nothing is created, and nothing is destroyed...
you were once a rock... you were minerals beneath the
water
tomorrow you will become the cloud, the river and the
air

the masters of paris
read big books
and turn over the leaves
but **suso**
you must read the living book
wherein everything lives

where dark is a way
and light is a place
where heaven that never was
nor will ever be
is always true

where an ever-written tablet
quenches the fiery shadow

for i have sat by thebes
below the wall
and walked
among the lowest of the dead

j then drew her long black hair out tight

and fiddled whisper music
as if on strings

never before had **suso** felt so sure of ancient times
he could almost smile
at those generations that wept for antiquity
as for a lost play
they would have liked to have parts in

now he was beginning to grasp
the dynamic significance
in later ages to form
a whole… and to be wholly past

supra quæ propítio ac seréno
vultu respícere dignéris: et accépta habére,
sícuti accépta habére dignátus

is it true
that there is a celestial half of life
as if fitted
to the semicircular bowl of earthly existence

could two full hemispheres fit together
to make one perfect golden orb

***suso** stripped a branch*
to make a flute
he threw a stone
at some small beast of prey

he stooped to the ground
and obliged a beetle to turn around
and the heavens passed over

where all sound ceased
a boundless void
an unhealed wound
in consciousness itself

j then spoke

a fool sees not the same tree
as a wise man sees
in your imagination
of which this world
is but a shadow

she took an atom out of space
and before his eyes
she opened its center
into infinitude

she ornamented it
with wondrous art
with her hands
she took a moment of time

the leaves silently breathed
and the stars beat like hearts
the infinite dark leaned
like water
against its outer surface

suso... what you believed
has vanished
the images beside you
and the world out there
these will unfold before you

open the imagery
and hand it back

j continued…
in a series originating in
and repeated to infinity
with alternating symptoms
of epicene comprehension and apprehension
nothing happens
that has not happened a million times before

peer back
and forward
peer through the ages
as they appear
in an instant
in one luminous moment
then you shall recover bit by bit
the lost scroll
and let the obscure texts
appear before you in their forms

i will command you to fracture them
just as the wind did to the sacred vase
and then i will teach you
to put them together again
in new ways

o' **j**
not even dante conceived
of my thoughts
the search for self…
through a labyrinth of time

the twists and turns
shrouded in the mists of memory
egolessness encounters
in this, my state of emptiness

where memories are pruned
blocked, and edited
filling the gaps
with things i believed to be true

as if of a sixth sense
self... in constant flux
morphed into a journey
through a labyrinth of labyrinths

entered through twists and turns
a sanctum sanctorum
viewed in shades of gray
through this lens of emptiness

a narrative
evolving over time
a god revealed only in my emptiness
among the rocks upon which i stand...

a garden forming in my mind
turned and rotated
where nothing's standing firmly

i wander through its corridors
hiding in a darkened street
visible yet unseen,
present but absent
animate but inanimate

covered in stillness
entrapped in a limitless void
i shall travel to this dimension
inexperienced and untouched

tonight i feel
i have arrived in a place
beyond books and rules
beyond scripture and dogma
to this... my uncharted path

let me alter my external
let me freeze in this moment
and stand still in a bottomless ocean
joined in a thirst for divine

transforming my inner energies...
i sit... as if this world now resides within me
i have exited the bondage
diving motionless into silence

where all is as nothingness
i now tread effortlessly beneath the waves
beneath turmoil and turbulence
there my body evaporates

from nothingness to light
my body disintegrates as my aura remains
and i will reach for a quiet song
where light will be my sound

an endless space before me
i lay silent in this spectral sea
where the equations and diagrams

become forces and magnitudes

i now sit inside this land of mysteries
inhabiting the body, rivers, winds and trees
where continents have been assembled as
constellations and galaxies dissipate
an ocean of truth stands naked and undiscovered
before me

VII

through the slow magic of time
customs arose...
and certain fear, discomfort and shame

conscience
and a moral sense
the work of a hundred centuries
and a billion minds

and fear
the first mother of the gods...
fear of death

aroused with myths and marvels
thunderbolt, aegis and trident
torches, snakes and thyrsuslances

the honors of a god
arose...
in a thousand forms

poetry embroidered magic
this offering
to harassed and bewildered men

a magic...
giving new form to human hope
the beginning of religion

suso reflects...

i looked over my shoulder... to a primitive time

where late in the evening, the burning fire's light
brightly shown
we nourished on the meat of our animal friends
and on occasion, a necessary one, we even ate our own

the thunderbolt and segis, the trident, torches and
snakes
attempting to block my every footstep... through the
slow mystery of time
everything became sanctified... even the poetry
embroidered magic
an unknown author sings out, proclaiming his myths
and marvels and rhymes

tightly folded and measured, let it be transformed
re-written in our prayer books and recited with beads
as we listen to ptahhotep, six-thousand guards stand
guard
protected from fear, there is no death... wrapped
securely in the armour of diomedes

we were born stoic, naïve and humble
and as buddha restated the words of isaiah
and confucious was formulating wisdom
power and strength was granted, even to the weakest
man in asia

culture hero, sacred king, is fear standing in the
shadow... is she our mother
who left the door ajar... how have we become sons of
the epicurean
and our daughters doubting even the upanishad
oh... the stories, they've been gathered, and claims

have been made of the day that the universe began

tightly folded and measured, let it be transformed
re-written in our prayer books and recited with beads
as we listen to ptahhotep, six-thousand guards stand
guard
protected from fear, there is no death… wrapped
securely in the armour of diomedes

j took **suso**'s hand…

and they walked along the shore
then off in the distance
was a faint appearance of a bearded old man
as they strode toward him…
he was unaware even of their presence
he appeared terribly distressed as he came closer

and all at once
there he was standing right in front of them
and, as if confessing a murder
he reached into his coat
and pulled out a thick notebook
and proclaimed
i am the **devil's chaplain…**
and here is my secret notebook

a notebook
which he had hidden for years
notes that would have been
damned by the church
as false, foul, atheistic, materialistic and immoral
and forbidden to be read by the faithful

the old man then put out his hand and said
i fear the words i have written
if made public
will crash the church
tear apart the moral fabric of society
and return the civilized to savagery

suso asked… may i see your notebook

as they sat together on the beach
suso perused the notebooks
for an indication
of what concerned this gentle old man

the first thing he read was
why does a bird's wing…
a man's hand and a bear's paw
have identical bones
even the same organs

as if they could be threaded in a chain

as **suso** read further the **chaplain's** notebook
there were sketches and descriptions
of how entire orchards sprang from one tree
and by extension species
all animals
shared one life force too

discoveries sketched
with broad geological brush-strokes

it became clear to **suso**
that for this tormented man

reason was divine
and progress its prophet
and he worshiped in the temple…
the temple of nature

as he thumbed page by page
suso exclaimed
these findings can no longer be hidden
they are crucial
to understanding the formation of life

that plant and animal kingdoms
had a common starting point
you have pushed ideas to their limits
starting a life-long trend
extrapolating from small origins
to big outcomes

the world…
an accumulation of tiny changes
everything natural, gradual and slow

the **chaplain** responded…
yes… nature works silently
it comes on the scene, making no claim… possesses
nothing
i try to understand… i stand back, feeling betrayed,
feeling mystified at this new sacred tome
whimsical protons and cells, hypothetical atoms and
genes, but i can't see a thing

the **chaplain** described the pain he caused his family
as he no longer joined them

in weekly worship at the family's church

i wish i could
believe the things they do
if they could only come inside my head
if they only knew

the mystery... the questions
all inside of me
if we must... i submit
it's divinity

i worship
at a church
they cannot understand

i have felt the awesome power
beneath the fragile crust
where the cathedral collapsed
and in the elemental forces
that raise and lower the continents...
forces that reduce man
even to insignificance
i began with devotion
to nature's god

but have now gone beyond that
to study nature
to explain its powers
understand its wisdom

and justify its ways
even searching beyond... for the laws of life
a search that i knew

would lead me into difficult waters

in pondering the divine
can he complain
that we can allow
satellites, planets, suns, universe
even whole systems of universes
to be governed by laws...

but even the smallest insect
we wish to be created at once
by special act

they say i am directly challenging
the supernatural laws of a creator god

o' this **devil's chaplain**
knew he was staring heresy in the face

as **suso** scanned his notebook further
he burst into a continuous series of notes
covering what must have been
at least a hundred pages in length
a breathless machine-gun-like effusion of telegraphic
jottings
representing hurried and exciting trains of thought
on the laws of life

the words that jumped form the page
were a total departure from radical wisdom
let alone religious convention

the **chaplain** explained
deep in this clandestine work

compiling notes that would shock the world
this was all too much for him
even his health is breaking

i have lived a double life
with double standards
unable to broach my discoveries
with anyone

i find myself lurching into unmitigated contempt
for the arrogance of my fellow scientists
for bending the universe to fit man
and then pronouncing a panegyric on god's design

my vision was no longer of a world
personally sustained
by a patrician god
but self-generated

a lawful redistribution of living matter
in response to
an orderly changing geological environment
even man, wonderful man
must collapse into natures wonderful cauldron

i reduced life to its starkest
to its living elements
to self-organizing atoms

in their eyes
i now doubt the sacred truths

ah… but a far grander idea
than the perverse idea

of god individually crafting
every slug and snail

i have to reveal my findings
cautiously, cryptically
and with trepidation… i will

my work was heresy to the geologists
and blasphemy to the parsons

my new gospel
explains mind, morality and belief…
the social development
of the human species

yet i shall be viewed as
the most despicable of men
the most arrogant, odious beast
that ever lived…
yes, i have become
the **devil's chaplain**

will my quest interrupt this struggle
as thy lust for heaven grows
and we sit atop a boundless sphere
whose center is everywhere, whose circumference is
nowhere

frightened by the eternal silence and endless space
i explore with presumption, perplexed and appalled
by the infinitely vast
and the infinitesimally small

j responded…

*o' **chaplain***
bless yourself with holy water
believe and be not dulled
here are prophets, just as you imagined
extracting sun for you... building your house from the
roof to the ground

but the **chaplain** interrupted...

do not look upon me with hope
don't pretend life has been given with consent
redeem the obscene from the slaughter
the thorns have been planted...
even the shield of my faith
has been broken

lines they come to me... texts, test tubes and
microscopes
yet i lay helpless and sleepless in this spectral sea
plotting equations and diagrams
measuring forces and magnitudes, peering inside a
land of mysteries

inhabiting the body, rivers, winds and trees
continents have been assembled
constellations and galaxies dissipate
an ocean of truth stands naked and undiscovered

invisible laws
unanswered prayers
matter attracting matter
delusions and crimes... and inverse squares

do not read my words

or come within four cubits of me
my unholy dogma is banned
predestination without theology
of poets, composers and saints
the odes of keats, the notes of hendel
is this the floor of the pantheon
or the ceiling of the cistine

as he turned and walked away
they saw the appearance of one tormented
worn and tired

a man who rushed in
where fools have dared to tread
never able to keep ahead
of the persecutor within

one unable to squeeze his discoveries
into the building of the church...

for the fault is not his
as blood that sees the light
and is drunk up by the earth
the forces of tradition
and of the ears of the deaf
have built invincible walls

the oblique star
the penetrating planet
hurled at him like a spear
an icy thunderbolt of cold fire
no longer in sight

suso and **j** reflect on the discoveries of the **chaplain**

suso now feels conflicted as he protests…
isn't the complexity of life
matched by the elegance of its design

i understand the world's resistance
it seems so hard to accept
it requires a very, very large leap
to believe that our trillions of cells
many very different from one another
can be organized with such precision…

ah… but **j** then interrupted **suso**'s thoughts
i shall take your mind on a journey
a journey of comprehension
a journey to the edge of space
the edge of time and understanding
where there is nothing that cannot be understood
and nothing that cannot be explained
even the illusion of design

we, the animals of the complex
in this universe, alone
one-trillion cells, molecules of complicated patterns
gaze upon my stature… at this machine of skin and
bone

i stand here, at the edge of space
where nothing is understood
yet all is explained
complexity, beauty and elegance… where nothing is
bad and nothing is good

stand close, behold the architects of his embroidered

web
grasp the absurd… suppose its intricacy
and over there… the marble has been piled
the parthenon stands before you
an unbroken fallacy

if time were our footsteps
and we walked until our shoes were broken and worn
how many steps 'til we confront our sister, lucy
take my hand, hold tight, before we get to bagdhad our
earth will have been born

yes, we are animals of complexity
in this universe, alone
one-trillion cells, molecules of complicated patterns
gaze upon my stature… at this machine of skin and
bone

the night's sky… colors filled with lifelessness, really?
where is thy carbon… make it suitable for life
stir them up… warm up the patterned molecules
turn them to crystals, cut off a piece and please give
me a slice

show me your dance
show me the snake's fang, and the orchid's protruding
flower
then replicate, multiplicate, mutate and hold on tight
and stir it up with every ingredient blended in tonight's
star-studded shower

then came evening… and morning
an eighth day

darkness to light... and truth
the present fixed beneath... and hailed beyond

thy kingdom has become one
carbon left explaining it all
complexity demystified
thoughts of the supernatural has come unbound

carbon... an enlightened equation
life
no longer explained in holy writ
magnificently presented in colored crayon

the chemicals react
obedient in their role
the clay-crystals enter the night
offer a regal bow, replicate and take their intended
position below

the invitations have been sent
all our guests have arrived, i thought there would be so
many more
the room is half empty... most of our friends will never
arrive
but slowly, gradually, this mystery has brought me to
your door

peer before the heavens
you who devise theories and elaborate schemes
in search of the answers... to questions never asked
unraveling innermost thoughts... of these complex
machines

yes, we are animals of complexity

in this universe, alone
one-trillion cells, molecules of complicated patterns
gaze upon my stature... at this machine of skin and
bone

oh, andromeda, two-million light-years away
oh, galaxy, so far in the distance of this deep dark sky
how do i see you, you have not yet even arrived
it's been five-billion years, our sun has not been
formed... how do i see you and why

a protostar slowly heats up
one-million degrees
another is exhausted... an unstable isotope
ah, but a star has been formed... get down on your
knees

the electron-positron appears
the universe is one second old
particles spontaneously created out of the vacuum
created out of nothing... or so i've been told

yes, we are animals of complexity
in this universe, alone
one-trillion cells, molecules of complicated patterns
gaze upon my stature... at this machine of skin and
bone

and this is what the **chaplain** understood

as **suso** reflects on **j**'s words
he muses...ah, that such complexity
evolved... with no designer

j said, oh **suso**
you misunderstand what the **chaplain** called
'natural selection'
it is not something that occurs randomly
rather it is nonrandom and cumulative

there is nothing special
about the substances
from which we are made
they are just collections of molecules
just like everything else

what is special
is that these molecules are put together
in much more complicated patterns
than the molecules of what many still believe
are nonliving things

they vibrate and throb and pulsate
and glow with living warmth
not because of a warm breath
or spark of life
rather, billions of discrete hereditary particles
carved in tablets of crystals
spontaneously formed
in the waters of our planet
with properties of replication
of multiplication heredity and mutation

suso replies… o' **j**… i think i understand…

but in this world of multiplicity
are we deprived of higher dimensions

does our mind refuse to inquire
into its own nature

have we been plunged
into the physical world
where all is veiled
across this space-woven cosmos

a fabric woven of light and darkness
where no shadow is cast
and darkness gazes in on itself
into the odorless, the tasteless and the voiceless

where self-questions reflect upon our essential core
then, in this moment of realization
we see through all eyes, we hear through all ears
and breathe through all breathing beings

j responds…

these lofty forms
yet i find them neither true nor false,
rather, like music… like a lyrical poem
a theory of beauty, of waking consciousness

all the symbols have been taught
let your visions be free, untrammeled
liberated, unconstrained… and divine
where once there was nothing… you now stand

VIII

suso stands perplexed
confused…

my mind… my thoughts
have been diluted
the intensity of your words
have become almost unendurable
what is the meaning of these words

they only appear to me
as if, from a strange book
a compound of fable
a symphony and nightmare
a monstrous enigma beckoning imperiously
from the shadowy pits of a dream

a very flesh-and-blood being
but nevertheless
a mythical and elusive one
as if little inhabitant lives
have been heaped in disorder

these words
they entered my ears
like phantoms
with pale pulverized voices

as if a naked flower
has been raised
over a dishonored land

with twisted eyelids
am i now
to pursue invented torments

geometry's inverted crystalware

as if beaten and bled to madness
and gorged by a fatuous god

o' **j**
let your words comfort me
who are you…
who are you **j**

i've been called a woman of fiction
a princess of the royal house of david
a writer…

yes, a writer

the mother of solomon
writer of words
words … censored, distorted and revised
by ancient priests and cultic scribes

i shall speak to you
you have come to sit beneath this tree
to demand the truth

listening …
you now only imagine
what i really mean

pater naster, qui es in caelis

i arose in the triumphant moment

of the establishment of a kingdom
one of millennium's past
yet my work is seen
as haunted by images of exile

i wrote:

rise, walk around on the land
a land open and broad
of the promise that reverberates
against the root of rehoboam's name

and again, i wrote:

i beheld the burden of the people
i come down to lift them out
to carry them to a broad, open land

yes, it was me who wrote…

of yaweh's molding of adam
to his digging of the grave for moses…
yes… the very heart of the torah

before a plant of the field was in earth…
before the wind of life
blew into its nostrils
and man became a creature of flesh
the sculpture modulated
from clay to flesh

i… the poet of so many words
wrote to remind them
that we sojourn in houses of clay
the dust… both as our origin

and as our destination

many have said that i gave them
a vision that had to be sealed…
or scaled down
or revised into moralism and belief

i… just a poet
the writer of many words
but it is they
that *censored, distorted and revised* my words

yes… it is true
my words are, but…
large rhythms of storytelling
that will take you down into egypt

down into the underworld
in apotropaic gestures
invoking archaic rituals
and ancient gestures
momentarily shrouded
by primitive magic

suso sits in stunned amazement
the scrolls… the scolls in the vase
did you write those words

j smiles

yes… but they had to be destroyed
the redactors scrambled them
to the point where the meaning was lost
and what has been left to mankind

is but mere childishness

that they were sealed in the vase
and that the vase crashed
and the scrolls lost
was my intent

the true words
will be re-written
but the final chapters
unscrambled and made clear

o' **suso**
i will replace them and repair the vase

and they shall be given to you

as the tablets given to moses
were smashed and replaced
so, my words will be re-written
and the scrolls re-opened

and i will chant the song
of the perpetual man
becoming and overcoming
the exuberance of being

the treasures of the imagination
of the rarest diamonds
are after all and shall be
only the pebbles and pearls
of an injured mollusk

but **suso**
no attempt will be made

to reduce their affect
from images to words
they will be left
to speak for themselves

through the eyes to the listening heart
voyaging through strange seas of thought
alone
of passion
that waits upon the touches
of the wind

it will always be the one
shapeshifting
yet a marvelous constant story

when i think
of how persistently
i, at one point kept going
strait ahead
in what appeared as a dream
it seems i must have known
there was something fine ahead
like the lovely grassy river
and the secure, high row of trees beyond

perhaps some of us have to go
through a dark place
before we can find
the river of peace
the clock must tick
and the pages
must be turned

the mysteries
whose secrets are written down
in the guarded libraries
of the great monasteries

may we reset
the intrusion of those prophets
who voiced its gospel
because they threw the icy water of doubt
upon our comfortable orthodoxies
which fed us with illusions
because much that is worthwhile
has been rejected by the compilers
and much that is printed
has been badly spoken

IX

Once again… an enormous wave
crashed onto the beach
and **suso** was swept in its wake

as he sank into deep choppy waters
the darkness covered him
and his breathing ceased

a fisherman's boat appeared
a hand reached out to him
and pulled him aboard

as **suso** sat wet, shivering and coughing
he looked up at the kind man that saved him
a man with soft eyes and a wizened appearance

this man stepped forward to offer
a warm blanket and some dry clothes to **suso**

once dried, warmed and changed
suso stood before this man
wearing an over-sized robe and soft leather boots
that the fisherman provided…

suso looked into his eyes
and saw in them an air of ease
and gentleness

i am **issa,** the fisherman said…
i have come
to provide a feeling of help

to the helpless
and the comfort of hope
to the hopeless

from the indus river
to ravalpindi
i ran over the pendjab
the land of the five rivers

i visited the golden temple of amritsa
the tomb of the king of pendjab
and turned toward kachmyr
the valley of eternal bliss
descended to the river djeloum
the waters of which flow gracefully
between rocky walls whose tops
reach the azure skies

it has been written
of my miracles
in artificial narrations
constructed from tradition

profoundly sedimented
into your imagination

yet my life…
is a painting
my acts shall be captured
as in a sculpture

the theological historians
have hidden me

the record of my
wandering years
is entirely missing

it's as though the mountains
are being undermined
exploded and shattered
by violent subterranean forces

yet, i must go forth

to the hidden chamber
draw my breath in tight...
enter into a mysteriousness
which lies within
so misinterpreted and misunderstood

enter the cave of stillness
ghostly in hidden meaning
o' those early tablets and texts
that unified mossa and thy bodhidharma
and me

open the doorways of senses
to words hidden for two-thousand years
despoiled motifs and gilded shrines
trampled appurtenances of enlightened ritual

to unravel the riddles of existence
the elementary principles
the antagonism between matter and mind
where realization's been darkened and veiled

and esoteric depths challenged

symbolic expressions and figurative phrases
grievously misinterpreted
through the dark outlines of a similitude

such are the varying fortunes of creeds
yet, we wait in time
to uncover its profoundest secret...
where resides a calm and intuitive wisdom

to study the way of dragons
in an ocean of a billion worlds
where no moment can be measured
where even trees are equal to you

yes... and the birds and rocks
are equal too...

leap beyond... wander at ease
let thoughts run like a wild horse
no longer chasing after words
taking the backward step

life is a mystery, not a question
a mystery to be danced
a twirling of concepts to unravel
dissolve into the cosmos
as you are no more
only existence is

so, man must
go ahead
and woman, make her wager
unravel the greater truths
provoke doubt... meet face to face

the mystery of thine own self
draw thy gaze inward
chant before the gentle amitābha
and the merciful kwannon...
feed this flame in thought

in these sensitive moments
perceive the sounds of the universe

here one will find thy being...
thy original face
before your parents were born

suso stood up
regained his balance in the rocky waters
as the boat swayed...

and looked into the fisherman's eyes
the appearance of his face
a walk of stature
a softness of a holy one
as one with a voice of authority

issa continued...

man and woman will always be in childhood
until they see and feel the grandeur of nature
and understands everything presented to their senses

they have always sought for tangible things
it was not possible for them to believe long
in that which escaped their material senses

and owing to the unreliability of human memory
historical facts about me, my travels

my life
that have been so embellished
by the oriental imagination
and it soon degenerated into fabulous legends

and yet still, the narrative realism
has become equated
with historical accuracy

and as texts merged with texts
and as events merged with citation
where anything began
and where it ended is now hidden

prophecy and history
began to interweave
influencing and even creating each other
the rephrasing prophetic allusion
telling the narrative
and inventing the history

ah… the creativity of mark
but those stories must be emphasized
for what they are
consummate theological fictions
magnificent theological fiction

ah… the first century
obscured from contemporary view
through the vagaries
of chance and fate

where we invent
mourn rather than mock

exaggerate and over-emphasize
distort, suppress and simplify

add magical prophets
and rewrite their responses
not with pens on paper
but with their blood and flesh

let us cross apocalyptic and sapiential
where they look for what is already there
not from knowing hidden mysteries
but from watching nature's rhythms

their error is in awaiting
rather than the seeking
in an abbreviated inspiration
of passion and descent

underlined in artificiality
hallowed within narrative frames
as sacred texts are adorned and merged
incarnated in painting and sculpture

hide the prophecy
tell the story
prophetize the history
and historicize the prophecy

this poetry embroidered magic
a universal myth in a thousand forms
born in superstition
aging in a chaos of experience

where glimpses of reality

lurk behind our scenes of thought
where an inability to escape
precedes the forces of the mind

deeply embedded in the human heart
secrets of eternally hidden wisdom
like a river
perpetually vanishing... within

superimposed and momentary
unconnected in a field of forces
where step by step, thoughts compress
beneath the depths of the unconscious

beyond desires
beyond memories and fears
where thoughts of self are shattered
where the illusion of you... is exposed

here the continuous and substantial
moments of emptiness
awe the human heart... and
your quest stretches out like an infinite line

here consciousness descends
and out of this absolute
time has ceased...
self is imagined... and each story is true

j appeared before the two men
how she did is unknown
yet she approached this man...
this fisherman...
she stood before him and bowed

he took her hand and smiled
and said

you desire to unravel the mysteries
to repair the shattered vase
and re-open the scrolls

you must be ready to touch life
at many sides

and you too shall speak to me
albeit in tones so low
that the world will sneeringly say
that we are deluding ourselves

but we shall both laugh pityingly
at the world
and forgive it

let us take nature as our tutor
to merge with our spirit
and into the absolute silence
of her surroundings
let every thought lapse away
into mere nothingness

i shall whisper
my heart-hidden secrets to you
and tell of those vanished scrolls

for the **chaplain** has told you
that truth depends
on the original abyss of radical amazement
that to him

science is the exclusive teacher of truth
it is here…
that radical amazement is enhanced

but your teachings tell us
that all beings are sacred

that to ignore
the sacredness of the forests, the rivers
the oceans, and the four-legged ones
is to crucify me all over again

suso now stands in shock
did you say 'crucify'

who are you

isso turns to **suso** and says

my cross is not a private, anthropocentric event
but a cosmic event
a rupture in the cosmos

and today
there is a culture, numb to the capacity
for reverence and awareness
of earth and her forests
her waters, fishes, animals, birds, trees
and the ground upon which we walk

intelligence can burst out
only from bits of stardust

yes, **suso**
we are rare and precious beyond calculation

but we are only possible
because of the composition
of the rest of the universe

to understand
and explore the deeper meanings
of doctrine and dogma
rites and rituals
even life and death

the treasure
has to be broken down
before it can be found
before the vase can be repaired
before the pieces will fit
once again
in their rightful place

man sees
but sees only the pieces
fixed in patterns

we must teach him to let go
of frozen minds
to enter deep into himself

let the images, vestiges and shadows
sink into the ocean and disappear
like the fable

cease your stretching after the shadow
let the profane
becomes sacred
let myths...

the truths of the human soul
stand outside their words
where there is silence
beyond stories of disdain

when you look at it
you cannot see it
it is formless

when you listen
you cannot hear
it is soundless

try to seize it
you cannot hold it
it is called subtle
take hold of reality
in its nakedness

i saw eternity the other night
driven by the spheres
like a vast shadow
and seven mornings heard them
but saw them not...

if the doors of perception were cleansed
everything would appear as it is

suso approached and bowed before **issa**...
and said...

for half a century i have endured hardship
and granted myself no rest
but have continually striven and investigated

and done as well and as much as i could

rejecting with a shrug of my shoulders
that brew of fantastic
and language perverting philosophies
that fanatical-purposive view of history
that carnival of all gods and myths
that romantics put together
those poetic fashions and insanities
born of intoxication

i have seen
imprisoned man beat upon the door
and broken into a dozen minds
that know nothing of each other

issa responded…

those imaginary words
those imaginary people
are created
out of the deepest
instinct of man

language has been
the instrument of controversy
and along the way
has grown abstract

as the painter, the mosaic worker
the illuminator of sacred books…
the illuminator of those pictures
out of old gospel books
are as sacred as the text

yet weaved all into one design
the work of many
though they seemed
the work of one

in the bhagavad gita
it states that god is everything
the hidden essence of all manifestation

let me, then
compose my thoughts
and silently repeat them
that i may find in the respite
gained by mental quiet
where nothing
and nobody external appears

henceforth in its pages
no event needs to be described
for it is now only
the story of a deepening stillness

what can one record of that sublime void
into which i seek to penetrate

the stormy winds are laid
roaring waves climb the distant rock
what dost thou behold, fair light
but thou dost smile and depart

the mask will dance
between columns of blood and numbers
between hurricanes of gold
and moans of poor souls

under a silence of a thousand ears
and tiny mouths of water
the mask will dance...
let the mask be free, let it dance

resonances within our innermost
the rapture of being

suso responds
when the cathedral is empty
when the crowds have stepped away
and i stand alone... crying out for meaning

stepping into the threshold of passage
where inner mysteries unfold
and the crowds have disappeared
and time and space stand in the dusk...
when suddenly, i am old

when stories stream by in kaleidoscopic form
i shall not escape...
but will i come to terms
searching through the ages... as they dance before my eyes
shattered, disintegrated and crushed... lying sweetly inside this holy urn

primitive and unsettled
etched on stained glass... spoken in timeless themes
and everything around me speaks
are these other people's words... or are they archetypal dreams

as candle lights flicker against the wall

dancing deep inside this cave
the eagle and serpent in an unending conflict
different costumes, different times, yet are all taken
from the same silent play

magical dragon, o' serpent with wings
has come out of the forest with your gold
inner mysteries magnified, treasure turned to ashes
tremendum et fascinans... i feel i am
but a dream of a shadow

issa reponds once more...

are you reading the world
where messages buried deep have been written to you
through ages in conflict
images ungrounded, as voices dance thy mystery tune
the dream is inexhaustible

an adventure awaits you... deep inside the dark forest
it is as if
you are so close to the edge, even the ground is shaking
into a world of fire...

the moon sheds its shadow, life sheds a generation
ah... the fascination and the terror
we have come as manifestations in this field of time
a shadow play over a timeless ground, a
misunderstood metaphor

then suso says

i am trapped in the image
of those facts that have been misread

it's a terrible mystery
in this foreground of wonder

issa responds…

a burst of magnificence
animals of reverence
painted caves… mythic imagination in still form
filling the landscape of my soul… with unintentional
consciousness

i am sitting inside this primitive cave
inside this cathedral… adorned in beauty unintended
the poet and the shaman, sing the song of the universe
the message is hidden, the pages have gone unread

i am climbing threads
i climb one, then i climb another
i have become small
stillness and movement are now bound together

i will fill thy heart
will you burst before me, and attempt to measure the
beauty of my soul
while i walk in secret, walk inside this night's burning
flame

suso then says…

i could not see you… were you there
i have spied on you when you claimed to be in secret
even captured your crown…
and let the night's gentle tone penetrate until the silent
echoes resonated

in the undulations, as harmony was carried away in
silence

are we expected to make ordinary judgments
the apparatus which allows us to understand limits...
eternal and infinite
yields to our blindness... we cannot know of their non-
existence

the gods, and for all they stood
have they not been simply swept away
or just taking refuge
or hiding in paint and hardening in their cast...
brushed and carved, and on bended knee we pray

why do you exist so eternal, so silent
how aimlessly your great spirit wanders
why do you spurn your heavens
o'... that which is to live immortally in song, in life...
must it flounder

why have you brought me to this place
in defiance of all divinity
where i am unfeeling, confused and selfless
have we come here in silence, to satisfy our wretched
needs

where we work without thinking
like the bird building its nest
looking neither forward nor back
isn't this the place where we were promised to be
blessed

in an inner chamber, draped and candlelit

a board of imitators still sit at the table
wearing dusty and worn symbolic objects
the chapel is empty, the alter is naked, all that has
been printed is exposed
o' holy fable

ritual play-acting, with swords and blindfolds
in toke of dazzlement by the light of wisdom
a theatrical odyssey...
might that which we call fate, be merely chance... has
thy kingdom come

for the muses are not executioners
thoughts ten times read
on paper ten times penned
on lead worn away... a blunt and leaden wit

seven cities disputing which had given you birth
the wolf has torn you apart... each can take its bite
life flows away and time brings us back
as we are today only once... tormented by the sea,
tormented by the night

is life but a closely guarded secret... in which the
manifest truth is what is hidden
where what we call fate is merely chance
and the only order is anagnoristic
then we look back, and find that our present has
quickly left us for the past

will there be shelter, will there be sustenance
for this lonely soul is still craving... still yearning
is there hope for another moment or just a memory of

the last
i will go back, open each page and step into the path
of my long toil of understanding

issa responds...

movement is time
stillness is eternity
there is a sphere known to the mind, hidden to the
senses
its center is everywhere, its edges are carved...
peer deep beneath this image of the axis mundi

gaze heavenward into the central mountain
the central mountain is everywhere
sacred groves clothe the night... erected as shrines
yes, you are lost in the forest...
turn your eyes inward, and fall to the ground

the feelings all around you are present
they echo inside
as nature tightly grips the calumet
you hold the stem to the sky

the sun breathes its first puff
you are standing on sacred ground
all temporal walls dissolve
my cathedral talks to me... listen... hear her sound

come to my cathedral
formed of majestic stone
stand with me in silence
a silence beyond sound... come to my home

to a transcendent unknown
where our shamans stand today
they are reaching out... the final secret is revealed
where the labyrinth penetrates... where the heart will
re-awake

like the wounded king
we'll not risk the adventure alone
our heroes have gone before us
the labyrinth is thoroughly known

follow the thread, travel outward
invent your magician
transform the giants
go forth, encounter your windmills... in poetic
imagination

fly the middle way
lest the sun melts your wings
lest the tides of the sea catch you
and be swallowed and crushed by waves forever
howling

you will wake in the morning and know
the questions hidden in our children's dreams
as if touched by time
where weapons were turned to flowers, in a world they
were just imagining

witnessing miracles like particles in the air
a man comes along... questions even the theory of sin
ah... the particles as they float
cluster tightly around and deep inside of him

there's a center of quietness within
which has to be known... reach out and hold
the penultimate truth
beyond words, beyond images... known but not having
been told

the lightning is thy child
thou art the seasons and the seas
having no beginning, with immanence abide
whereof all things are born, breathe and be free

your god is everywhere
attis, adonis, gilgamesh, osiris
as with the moon
in just thirty days you will rise

in this universe of violence
the furnaces roar
look to the stars, reach to the sun
even tonight, circling planets are being born

from distances beyond
littered with dust and gas
sounds from a billion years ago
i hear your murmurs and explosions, the alpha and
omega, the first and the last

the sand painted image
cosmic images redrawn
forces from the depth of consciousness
desireless and fearless... the world has already become

the monster comes through
vishnu appears

the universe is destroyed
first with fire, and then torrential flood... what is left,
but ashes and tears

shiva... standing in circles of flames
burns away the veil of time
the drum of time, the tick of time
time explodes... what you thought was the future now
stands before you as history maligned

the original meaning
prophets and angels read to us in stories
carved and chiseled from stone
the stories, the mysteries... the fantasies

go past the words
go within, stand naked and unconscious
past every word, every song, every motif
experience the radiance, the essence... the fullness

magical dragon, o' serpent with wings
you've come out of the forest with your gold
inner mysteries magnified, treasure turned to ashes
tremendum et fascinans... you are but a dream of a
shadow

issa then touched suso's head
turned and walked away

suso and j watched...

his fair-moving on the plain
but his bright form lasted not
the sun-beam fled from the sea

and he was seen no more
he sailed away
as grey mist before the wind

as **issa** moved beyond their sight
suso exclaimed
who was that man

perplexed he walked along the beach
in silence

with **j** at his side
neither spoke until they came upon two men
sitting by a fire... looking beyond and through them
as if talking
but there were no words

dóminus vobíscum
et cum spíritu tuo.

X

the names of the two men were unknown to **suso**
but not to **j**
they too, had written sacred words
as she had done... so many years ago

nagarjuna and **ashu** stood and bowed
as **suso** and **j** approached their site...
it was as though they knew **j**

ashu began to speak

imaginary people
are created
out of the deepest
instinct of man

we are now in the age
where there is nothing but words
footprints
symbols distilled and enriched
by the imagination

but we can do nothing with these words
we must turn away from them
and go back to the source
where all things began

as if the spirit slowly descends
from its celestial place
to the level of intelligent thought

then he sighed

o' that there were heavenly paths
by which to steal into another existence
into happiness

just then **suso** exclaimed...

do no the sacred texts
direct us to that path

nagarjuna waved his hand before them
and said...
let it not be inferred
that such a path exists
nor that it does not
nor both, nor neither

all that is compounded
becomes uncompounded
for there is no cause
no arising, no enduring, and no ceasing

the 'i' arises
dependent upon bodily aggregates
it is in fact nothing
but the reflection of a face

the cosmos is seen as real
by those who are far away
but it is not seen as real
by those who draw near to reality

just then **ashu** interrupted...

but is the certain
worth more than the uncertain
the illusion
more valuable than truth

yet, without a constant counterfeiting
of the world
by means of these paths
man could not live

so, we must dance in our chains
and between our swords
it is none the less true
that more often we gnash our teeth
and are impatient
at the secret hardship of our lot

may its glance someday
overspread like a gilded, blue, mocking twilight
this aging civilization
with its dull gloomy seriousness

but as we are today
the wild beast
has not been slain
it lives, it flourishes
it has only been transfigured

nagarjuna then speaks...

the real world
is different from our ideas
which are just our thoughts

we create pictures of reality
within our minds
and then tend to believe
our own mental constructs...

suso has been listening intently
and then he asks...

are not our thoughts
real entities
that actually exist in the world

nagarjuna responds...

we tend to believe
that even solid matter is a concept...
but what we call matter
is nothing more than stimuli
within our own sense organs
as interpreted by our brains

mind and matter are
in the final analysis
the very same thing...

ashu vehemently disagrees

you want to have a dialogue with the stars

climbing upon false broken words
and false rainbows
between false heavens
crawling and creeping

no path anymore

only an abyss and deadly silence
i know you want this
but from this path
your will has strayed

but truth is not a toy
you cannot get it ready-made
there is no factory that manufactures it
and there is no market where it is available

you will have to search for it
in the deepest silences of your own heart
and except you
nobody else can go there

ashu continues…

suso, you must put aside your knowledge
because it is all borrowed
put aside your god
because it is only a belief
and nothing more

put aside the idea
of any heaven or hell
because they are only
your greed and your fear

be as the adventurer
who goes into the unknown
on the untrodden path
without any fear

go…

where there are no longer others
to one life
in millions of manifestations
in the trees, in the animals
in human beings
in the stars
these are all manifestations of one life
one single life

be a wanderer of the soul
be a wanderer
in the innermost depths of consciousness

suso bows his head
walks away in despair
from those words that ended in
an emptiness without cause

uninitiated actions
an actor with no action
a world
unarisen and unceased

entities of impermanence
deceptive
hollow, empty

as if all has disappeared
and there is only a pure sky
a pure isness... utterly innocent
with no clouds of knowledge

it has become late
he lies down

looks up to the sky
a sky full of stars

as **suso** falls into a deep sleep he says

i must climb above myself
up and beyond
until i have even those stars under me
beyond this fable-song of madness

and not let my learning
lead to the dogmatic
allow time to hone, focus
and widen my understanding of the world

i must begin at the beginning...
the indivisible particles
the building blocks of the world

do they really exist
or are they just concepts
that help us understand reality

understand both things
as they appear
and their ultimate existence
their true nature

as **suso**'s eyes became heavy... he drifted off
and in this dream state his thoughts continued...

it has always been argued
that objects have an intrinsic existence
governed by laws of cause and effect

but today… such ideas
are being seriously undermined
the idea that the basic ingredients of matter
have a definite existence

just like **nagarjuna**'s idea of emptiness

but, what does emptiness mean
the things we see around us
the phenomena of our world
do they actually lack
solid existence

i need to understand…

but the words they speak
contradict all that i see
ah… shall i close my eyes and let the blindness prevail
partake in thy consecrated meal… close my eyes and
drop to my knee

and **suso** fell into a deep sleep
but his mind kept turning on and off …

let the night create one thousand monsters
ten-thousand-fold will be my counter rage
my spirit will become an all-consuming fire
you will not divide me from myself, i will stand and be
shaped in my own image

may my whole heart melt away into this fire
i will watch, i will listen…
a new world may emerge, yet i will not be consumed
suffer, weep, and i will disregard you as you do i

i will find a rock and make a new castle of ten-thousand rooms

i will run for shelter, scream for just one morsel, a falling crumb
for this lonely soul is still craving… still yearning
is there hope for another moment or just a memory of the last
i will go back, open each page and step into the path of thy long toil of understanding

lying, curled in on myself
this… my pose for the years
my quest and my retreating soul
never until this moment have i been under your spell
eating this bread while drenched in my tears

is there still power in me to bear
that i could flee to be with you, on this day
dispossessed of my dearest need
will you give me more than you have given before
i move up, i move down, weave to and fro… in these floods of life, in this storm of deeds

in the end
what is life… what is death
shifting sands… of an eternal sea
i am captured in this loom of time, a guilt-drenched wretch

an eternal sea
arching sky above
garment of divinity

i have no name for you... do you come in hate, or is
this just another distorted façade disguised as love

will there be shelter, will there be sustenance
for this lonely soul is still craving... still yearning
is there hope for another moment or just a memory of
the last
i will go back, open each page and step into the path of
thy long toil of understanding

yet in his dream-state, he saw
in a darkened corner, there sat **j**
under candlelight and her egyptian reed pen

suso could see over her shoulder
each of the words she wrote
as she chants the song
of perpetual becoming and overcoming

the chant o' the dynamic yahweh
the exhuberance of being

there is always yahweh...

and **j** created him as she wrote...

before a plant of the field was on earth
before a grain of the field sprouted
he made the earth and sky
a mist from within
would arise to moisten the surface

in the beginning
he created the heaven and the earth
and the earth was without form

and void; and darkness was *upon the face of the deep*
and his spirit moved upon the face of the waters
and he said

let there be light
and there was light
and yahweh saw the light
that it was *good*

and the evening and the morning
the first day

suso looked into her eyes as she wrote
and he saw...
the center of the universe
gravity explaining the infinite
a day without yesterday
an initial burst of matter and energy
coalesced atoms
creating and mysteriously forming the stars
measuring time and space
the beginning

and then
a thin film of life
on this obscure and solitary lump of rock and metal

it was all coming together in this dream
in his mind

and as **j** continued to write
words were filling a large glass object
hiding behind her shadow

a thin film of life
a lonely speck
in the great enveloping cosmic dark

the stars and the carbon they make
is this the secret
ah...
we are made of stars

violent and exploding
billions upon billions
scattering
each a burning star

blowing to pieces
littering with dust and gas

planets being born
planets busy dying
there came murmurs, microwaves
echoes of explosions

the primeval atom
the extragalactic nebulae
a single quantum
a burst of fireworks
hot burning embers
and galaxies moving away

the beginning of time
the day without yesterday

when **suso** awoke
she was gone

or was he just dreaming

he rushed to the corner of the room
where **j** was writing
there was no reed pen
no papyrus that she wrote upon
and no glass container in the corner
holding her words

he rushed toward the beach
looked off in the distance
she was gone

so **suso** sat on a rock
trying to make sense of this dream

the words were still in his head
he could still see every word that she wrote

words that startled
readers from many thousand years ago

from...
before a plant of the field was on earth
before a grain of the field sprouted
before there was the earth and the sky

to...
the beginning of time
the day without yesterday

he lowered his head and softly spoke to **j**... wherever
she might be

i followed you through evenings and alleyways

they hovered over me ...
crowded in deepness in a series of disconnected facts
my imagination is not to be trusted
the hallway leading to the stairway is dark and endless

oh, the degree of comfort we have received
are they illusion of understanding
are they imaginary forces
that we are inventing

XI

suso heard a voice
the voice of an older man
a voice he did not recognize

he looked up and saw
him walking barefoot in the sand
skipping stones across the water as he walked
all the while talking to the seagulls and the crabs

suso wondered
who is this man
where is he from

suddenly, by his side
the appearance of an old priest
grave and imperturbable
with upturned eyes
his face more ennobled
still… with reverent mood

he approached **suso**
looked deeply into his eyes
and said…

you look perplexed young man
may i be of any assistance
and he crossed his legs
and sat on the sand

although surprised at the man's inquiry
he felt a burning need to tell someone

about last night… about the dream
or was it even a dream…

and he began telling the man
of the events of last evening
and the writings of **j**

when **suso** finished
the man reached down
and grabbed a handful of sand
as he held it out, he explained

the sand, rocks, water, and air
they are all just vibrating molecules and atoms
interacting and inter-connected
creating and destroying one another

he then pointed skyward and said

see the cascades of energy coming down
in which particles are being created and destroyed
in rhythmic pulses

this is what your friend **j**
was writing about
a work so comprehensive
and so universal
that the entire bible and koran
could be founded upon it

just then **suso** felt a rush running through his body
as though the elements
were participating in a cosmic dance of energy
it was as if he felt its rhythm and heard its sound

the man continued

heraclitus taught that all changes in the world
arise from the dynamic and a circle
an interplay of opposites
opposites as a unity
which contain and transcend all

ah… existence is a dance
the attempt to grasp reality becomes an excursion
you are going nowhere in a timeless moment
in this, my poem of empty space is sung in a
surrounding silence

in statements of ultimate things
sung in a suggestive form of myth
where language is confused…
here, i have discarded all the words with which i
thought

i will throw a pebble into the pool of every listener's
mind
where a deep, illimitable quietude descends
where a long fall of snow, swallows all sounds
where mind is overlaid with the wind and the waves

where a piece of life has been deliberately broken off
and wrenched away from the universe
appearing to drop off all by itself…
it reappears… turn slowly
discover the whole cosmos is now inside of you

where we try to measure, analyze, and classify
and interpret the world by grasping little pieces of it

the self will fall away in this moment
here is where we find that it has vanished like the past

and **suso** saw the atoms of
and at that moment
he saw the dance of shiva

the old man continued

and you, my son
must transcend the notion
of being an isolated individual self

to see the cosmos
as one inseparable reality
forever in motion, alive, organic
spiritual and material at the same time

the divine is not that of a ruler
who directs the world from above
but of a principle
that controls everything from within

ah… but the city
is not to be found in nature
rather the embodiment of the human kingdom
is of the imagination

here… time is unwound

no one sleeps in the sky
no one
every rumor will be stone
and every footprint, a pulse

here the impassive faces
they row under
to where they speak to each other
across time and language

and they echo each other

i am in nature
and nature is in me
as soon as a name is given
the divine ceases to be divine

the old man stood and bowed to **suso**
he simply said; i am **los**
and walked away
barefoot in the sand
waves softly gliding over his feet

again, **suso** could hear him
talking to the gulls and the crabs

then as if
fourteen suns had passed
and he had faintly journey'd
o'er his dark abode
j returned

his food, she brought in iron baskets
his drink in cups of iron too

she saw the tears on his face
then she too burst into a virgin cry

to **suso**
her words, a shadow of prophecy

shivering along by the sand and the shells
whispered across the ocean
as beneath the ruins
where their sullen flames faded

in a statue-like pose
she now hovered above him

in her pose, she sang
he heard the definite tones

they stood at length
and parted
amid that columnar circuit
of the sand and sea
beneath the last twilight of starless skies

suso stood gazing
as if on a vacant seat
in an empty hall

on a sanctuary
with no presence to hallow it
and heaven left empty

an imagination that revealed a subtlety
inaccessible by any sort of lens
but tracked in that outer darkness
through long pathways, devoid of sequence
devoid of an inward light

the last refinement of energy
incapable of bathing even the ethereal atoms
hidden deeply beyond...

a sacred illuminated space

suso began to walk away

in her soft commanding voice, **j** said

suso… you must stay

there is no need for you to leave
stay and listen
don't even listen
just wait
don't even wait
be completely quiet and alone

the world will offer itself to you
to be unmasked
it can't do otherwise
in raptures it will writhe before you

j's finger wrote in the sand
then she wept
then rose as if renewed
in zeal and awe

again, i tread the streets
after four-thousand years
nothing is final, she chants
no man shall see the end
he does not know how old he is already
or how young he is still going to be

we walk through ourselves
meeting robbers, ghosts, giants
old men, young men, wives

widows and brothers-in-law
but in the end
always meeting ourselves

they both look up
heard the foot steps
swashing beneath him
the old man returned

the moonlight shown upon his face
now clothed in a garment of solitude
every little particle of light and air
became opaque black and immense
as it shown on his shadowy face

he spoke of strange things

a rock of difficulty
and a cliff of black despair
that the immortal wings labored
against cliff after cliff
and over valleys of despair

he took off his garments of cloth
and clothed himself with imagination
and even in his words
there appeared a void
outside of existence

cross the boundary of your consciousness
become a valley
hold an entire mountain in your lap
touch the infinite... now let silence speak

wrap up and label the sky
until the throne of what you thought was the absolute...
is left vacant
now turn inward beyond all dimensions

reach out and stretch further
drift, as if you are attached to nothing
you are standing two inches off the ground
your mind is frozen... flesh and bones all melted
together

your tongue now paralyzed by its own revelation
a varied world of nature vanishes from your sight
it merges in a boundless ocean of luminous space
as vanishing hands are clutching at the clouds

to this... a state of consciousness without
differentiation
devoid of the knower, the knowing and the known
an evening by the river, a jewel of mystical imagination
and here you will cross the khajou bridge... where no
railings are needed

j sat at the water's edge
her hair unbound
her feet naked
tears running down her face

her thoughts...
her reason growing
like the wheel of a hand's
incessant turning

day and night without rest
as she raved upon the winds
left to the trampling foot
and the spurning heel

the divine never touches human life
without upsetting that natural order
like a bird... caged without a door
frantically trying to clutch the world
in its net of abstractions
in dimensions beyond all contradictions

bound and fitted, as if being obscure...
from the moon, gendered from your mind
and from our eyes... as if giving birth to the sun

thought scatters our mind within this posture
where interpretations of reality are found
veiled behind the arbitrary meanings
o' you, my detached philosopher

studying life from a distance
artistically framed...
through metaphor and irony
obliterate the meanings,

right there
existence stands before me

j stands and says

i must go
uncertain of my fate
but i shall return

this is thy hour o' soul
thy free flight into the wordless
the day erased
the lesson done

thee fully forth
emerging, silent, gazing
pondering

suso now wandering and confused
lost to himself
ill-assorted, contradictory
pausing, gazing, bending, and stopping

the powerful quartet
of night and the sea
the soul or unknown nature
the other that i am

he says...
let me glide noiselessly forth
with the key of softness
to unlock the locks
with a whisper

set open the door o' soul

alone in the woods, the water and the sky
in silence, i will tell you my loves and dreams and lies
i sit undisturbed, my legs are crossed
imagining the moods of nature, trees staring back...
my mind is lost

i fell asleep while demons swarmed about my head

i dreamed of reason, i dreamed of monsters, of
darkness and dread
i saw a man lying naked and stretched upon a rack
said he discovered that the earth is moving... and that
deep in the sky, no one's looking back

he cast his eyes upon the globe
bishops stood before him... beards were burning, all
wearing darkened robes
pursuing history in volumes... asking for proof, for
solace in his grief
for comfort and sustenance and healing from terrible
defeats

per huius aquæ et vini mysté-rium eius
efficiámur divinitátis consórtes,

XII

i walked to church
father grabbed my hand
mama sang the moment
i absorbed the meaning

i, the enlightened one
when heaven was young

can **suso** find a way
to rescue his learning
from the crumbling medieval architecture
of his mother's church

for not only have all the old mythic notions
of the nature of the cosmos gone to pieces
along with them
the symbolic forms
the supports of civilizations
the universally cherished figures
of the mythic imagination
the facts of the mind
our psychological order of dreams

the wisdom of our species...
fixed in patterns of archaic feeling

lined in orderly patterns
everything understood
it was all explained to me
i absorbed the meaning

i the enlightened one
when heaven was young

he turned to **j** and bowed his head

with pen in hand
in a movement of her hands
j furthered in her verse
and shuddered so...

rhythmic verses overlaid with wind and waves
merged in a boundless ocean of luminous space
as if a pebble is thrown into the pool of your mind
where your sense of self no longer exists

enter this empty space of surrounding silence
beyond all naturally occurring forms
concealed by the workings of the mind

yahweh's finger wrote the law
then wept
then rose in zeal and awe

in the newtonian voids
between the substances of creation
provinces and empires of chaos
invisible to this creature, man
sat chaos beneath

having penned such
j became as a little girl

woven
into the garment of the body
woven with care

her words...
the sacred words of milleniums

rocks of solid fire and ice valleys
plains of burning sand
of rivers, cataracts and lakes of fire
in this land, darkness flamed...
no light and no repose

as she then turned to a fresh reading
of these words
she felt, upon a depth of reflection
that she should perhaps have rewritten
her book of the psalms with **prince arjuna** in mind

ah...
she was glad
that she had not done so

to regard as a religious sentiment
to a mystery beyond thought
to the point that the mystery
is transcendent of categories
of names and forms
of sentiments and thought
is realized as the ground of one's own very being

*you, my dear **svetaketu***
you are it
o seeker of knowledge
from ignorance
to the knowledge of self

*dear **svetaketu***

when breathing
you became breath
when speaking, voice
when seeing, the eye
when hearing, the ear
when thinking, the mind

you turned the magic
into art
even the ultimate form
of wisdom
on the marbles of the floor
where immortals meet immortal

where the most intimate
hidden mysteries
are not defined for you
in terms contrived

where a contemplation of the cross
the odor of incense
hieratic attires
the tones of gregorian chants
the kyries
heard and unheard consecrations

it is here...
that we shall we dance

what is good and what is evil
true and false
right and wrong
in which dichotomies are dissolved

in the metaphysical impulse of compassion
and, if excluded from heaven
are sanctified in hell

j in deep reflection
writes…

o' master of labyrinths
and of mirrors
are we not mere fragments
of you, o god
who, at the beginning of time
destroyed yourself
in a desire for nonexistence

i have venerated
my gradual invention of you
also, of heaven and hell
ah… are they not
but admirable and curious designs
of our imagination

down deep into the darkness
into the mystery, into the shadow
into the forgotten parts of ourselves
a void of inexhaustible content
one mirror reflecting another
with no shadow between

but this weaving
of thought and feeling
brutally disrupting
whose motions within the room

most faintly apprehend
scalded with emptiness

i denounce the conspiracy
of those deserted offices
swept clean of agony
that erase the designs of the forest

where green sunflowers tremble
in the wilderness of dusk
and the sky is stripped naked
while the planets rust

let me tell you about life
the meaning and the end
the life
which throbs through my veins
which runs in the sap of the plant

let me re-write the sentences
torn from the vase
of a texture
midway between life and books

and find but the secret passage
within the mind
that will lead thee
to thy hidden chamber
within thine own soul

j looked heavenward
and smiled

nagarjuna returns...

lights a fire in the sand
stares into her eyes
as his thoughts flow
she stares
leaning, hushing…
the tide closing in

under the moonlight
under the brush, her hair
in her familiar breath
she sets her pen
to a blank scroll
and in the press of twenty thousand thoughts

lyrics are written
unrecognizable
words unredacted and unrevised
convoluted, yet lofty in form

clarifying insights give way
retrieving the shape of man
from behind this artificial wall
where lies a reality unknown

infinite and complex
multidimensional with no straight lines
no regular shapes
where nothing happens in sequence

as she writes
she does so, using metaphors and symbols
poetic images, and allegories
often full of magic

never precise
her myths embody
a truth that cannot be stated in words
where things and events
are realities of nature
are an illusion
where the external world and inner world
are two sides
woven into an inseparable net
of endless, mutually conditioned relations

nagarjuna watches her intently
he reaches and touches her hand
she stops and lays down her pen
as **nagarjuna** speaks

as you re-write these sacred scrolls
it is just as if you were to break open
a single mote of dust

it shall reveal
a billion rolls of sutras
and the sands of the ganges
will be realized
in an instant of thought

then pouring a mysterious sign over the sand
he continued…

is this, the mandate of reverence
where the sense of existence occurs
then… take my hand
let us enter the relatively unknown

and discover a sphere of unconsciousness
the dimensions of experience
that we barely suspected even exist

here, the drama will unfold...

in a constant rumble of feelings
acquire a sense of distance from the body
enacting on the stage of our inner theater
as the mind surges beneath a billowy sea

beneath the apparent stillness
into a vast interconnectedness... a forerunner to
thought
here you will cleave inwardly to sounds unimpeded
and lyrical
shining forth in solitary splendor

and the rain will fall
the conquest will begin
what was dis-orientated and disruptive
in a mirror of conditioned existence... will become
archaic

re-framed in a different picture
an outer wrapping superimposed
contradicting discarded and musty thoughts
where waves of being once came in conflict

thoughts now playing the music of the spheres
in an uninterrupted continuum as in an unbounded
ocean...
collapsing the inner architecture
surrendered in silence

but the truth is thy symbols
and as you write
you must see into their meaning
and discard all the historical
all existential encumbrances

archaeology is silent
hanging its head in secret shame
for it has had to withdraw
those guesses and theories
dressed up as though inspired

spend a night's vigil
and watch the world with the sphinx
the very spirit of solitude

the spirits
of vanished priests
and departed kings
flit to and fro
across their ancient haunts
like living shadows
without substance

let body and mind
slip into
the most quiescent state
shrouded in mystery
rooted in obscurity
more ignorant of itself
than of anything else

interpreting human experience

without preconceptions
be amazed
and you will understand

your words
will penetrate the veil

reality will be seen
interdependent
even at the subatomic level

what happens here on our earth
is decided by all the vast cosmos
what occurs on our tiny planet
depends on all of the universe's structures
an understanding of interdependence
should demolish the wall of illusions
that our minds have built up
between ourself and others

the world thus appears
as a complicated tissue of events
alternating or overlapping or combining...
thereby determining the texture of the whole

nothing
including matter and mind
intrinsically exists

through the empty branches
the sky remains

we are an empty awareness
that can watch identity rehearsing itself

in thoughts and memories relentlessly coming and
going
ripened until it is real
and they come toward you
to meet and to be met

suddenly, and in a radical way
this demolition of concepts and assumptions has
begun
that very sky is taken inside us physically

as **j** listens intently
she becomes perplexed

she stretches her dark body far
but look— back there
j's twin spires gleam up high
as if through those two points of feeling
as if she were sucking in the violet ink of sky

nagarjuna pauses… and with a smile explains

things do not exist in absolute terms
but do nevertheless exist
their nature must be sought
in the relationships that bring them together

but their solidity
is a mere illusion

primal experience takes place, as it were
within a world soul
a living matrix of embodied meaning
endowed with symbolic, archetypal significance

that flows between inner and outer
between self and world

but how is this so, **j** asks

am i falcon, a storm
or am i a great song
a living matrix of embodied meanings

nagajuna continues…

when the thrones are disassembled
and thy country limps into the endangered shadow
where blades of grass once pierced the night
and fiery cannonballs lit the sky in a mighty show

as you lay staring at jupiter's galilean moons
sandleless you shall stand before jove in craving silence
ageless you shall become the motion of the seas
until destinations are moved where our kings once
inflicted damages in recompense

you shall wander in the woods
you shall adore the sun
you shall swim in crystal lakes and climb to heights
unimagined

bow your head, close your eyes… it has begun

i have heard a thousand cries
of mouths opened wide and eyes closed in narrowness
and whispers from ten-thousand forms
having gained entrance to your thoughts, i sit stunned
and motionless

the unintelligible things you shall behold
in wonder... you will really think these things
let the moon shine and watch your mind decompose
the mansion that you once occupied is now missing its
king

you shall wander in the woods
you shall adore the sun
you shall swim in crystal lakes and climb to heights
unimagined

bow your head, close your eyes... it has begun

through the vastness
and the changes in form
spiraling upwards in cycles
something rich and strange is being born

on infinite levels, they collude and conspire
hidden forces compete through the tiers of time
the beauty and elegance... the simplicity
the ladder stands before you, step forward and climb

minds intently seeking patterns
through quirks, oddities and pathways to change
in a state of acknowledged ignorance
as if history's been disassembled, shuffled and
rearranged

a hundred-million years
demons of effectiveness
adding up all that is good
the hand of time has marked the ages

the perception of solid reality
is caused by the momentary stabilization
of a network of relationships

threads that we can reduce to fibers
then to molecules
then to atoms
and finally to particles whose mass
is equivalent to intangible energy

j responds… but **nagarjuna**
but how do your words relate to the sacred scrolls
that i must re-write…

he responds…

what has already been written
is the writing of ordinary prose
page after page
lacking understanding
breaking like the sunrise
just as a savage looks at a ship
rejected, overturned and despised
the usual price is paid
for the failure to grasp
excitements that lead to nowhere

o' j, time's an illusion…
lest we forget to laugh

at each infinitesimal moment
everything that seems to exist changes
this is so
once we have recognized that change is inevitable

and omnipresent

you, **j** must write
that all can understand that the universe
is not made up of solid, distinct entities
but of a dynamic flow of incessant interactions…

a trio of vibrating strings

as musicians charm us
by vibrations strings…
the strings sing and vibrate
all around us

and the universe is in fact a vast symphony
this orchestrated, synchronous activity
of large, discrete sets of neurons
among the hundreds of billions
creating an emergent state
a state of consciousness of time

we have the sensation of now
of a present with a duration
but this synchronization
produces a succession of emergent states
they then give us the sensation of time

but through your words of understanding
they will come to know…
the past and future have no reality
and the present is ungraspable

things seem to happen
in the world of appearances

as cause and effect
yet...
they have no intrinsicity

thus consciousness
and the world of apparent phenomena
are linked by interdependence
forming our perceived world

there is no distinction
the material and immaterial
the distinction between the interior world of thought
and exterior physical reality is a mere illusion

mental events, discursive thought
hope and doubt
the impulses and reasoning
are all part of ignorance and illusion

we become lost
in the tides of thought
in a magical world
where mythological images reflect the complex

where our ancients
saw the sun spirit
shed light on the earth spirit
and the tree, flower, and river spirits
during the day

the moon spirit
illumined the night
the inanimate world personified

you see **j**
we have formulated laws
in terms of equations, numbers
relations and correspondences
but structures result from conceptual thought
with no inherent existence

the mind distorts and creates illusory walls and doors
and then create illusory keys
revealing a million bewilderingly mysterious forms
and in the end... exposes a limitless ocean of emptiness

so...
sit secretly inside the present
drown inside the ocean of being
leap beyond the boundary of awakening

imagine what you were before you were even born
yield the grip
of twirling and unraveling concepts
leap beyond the boundary of delusion

free from the paths unconstrained by ordinary
thinking
abandon a mind that merely thinks in words
and chases after words to undo words
take the backward step and turn inward

tame your thoughts
of paths that run like wild horses
leap beyond the boundary of delusion
enter into a particle of dust... and there construct a
treasure king's land

in a circular form the blossom is full
in the ocean of a billion worlds… where all things are
linked
where no moment can be measured
attain it even for a myriad eon… a thousand lifetimes

in stillness, where mind and object merge
go beyond enlightenment
study the way of dragon and dugong
in an ocean of awakening

descend into deep chasms
reach the ground of no-doubt
disappear forever behind the mountain.
confront naked existence, lift the veil… let the trees
float

let this veneer melt
and the magic revealed
once concealed behind layers of meanings…
the masks shall be unveiled

j picks up her pen
and began to write…

thoughts
they have no shape
no color, no position
and that they fade away
they come from nowhere
and have nowhere to go
when they vanish

their solid appearance

melts like frost in the sun
remain therefore
in the mind's primordial simplicity

the natural clarity of the present moment
the immutable serenity
of the mind's ultimate transparency
without the past or imagining the future
and without hope or fear

the world…
a vast stream of events and currents
interconnected and interacting

aristotle's immutable heavens
and newton's static universe are no more

suso continued to sit
close to **j**'s side
reading every word
listening to every saying
every thought she has had

yet he now felt

completely quiet and alone
as the world offered itself
to be unmasked

he knew

it could not do otherwise
in raptures it will writhe

he had entered that place

directly opposite experience
where all that he had been taught
now shifted into the unconscious
into a field of action
of which he knew nothing

and the deeper he went
the more he wanted
to be closer to the final realization
but the resistance grew heavier
like coming down to those areas
the ones that are repressed
that you have to pass through

will this be
where the magic is
where enlightenment shows the way

suso… is emigrating
to an unknown
undiscovered land

pater naster, qui es in caelis

suso again dwells in a darkness
but… does this darkness hold promise of a dawn

the scrolls were taken from him
now as he watches **j**
he feels every word from her pen
every conscious thought
as if her breath
is re-writing each truth

is the world ready
for these words to be revealed

he feels a detachment
a withdrawal
a radical transfer of emphasis
from the external to the internal
a retreat from the desperations of the waste land
to the peace of the realm that is within

will there be a moment
when the walls of the world
seem to open for a second time
into the dark
where the jewels glow
where the mysteries of the energies
pour through him

like a harsh, clawing plant
of linked and bitter leaves

they now pierce
his separations to the depths
extinguishing his power

and spreading his grief

around him
the sound of night
the day, the month, the time

the sound of the gentle dawn
waking in the abandoned sea
lined with its rags of absence

a ring chained to space
clouds, spheres that touches
hurtling the mute waters

they surge ahead
overtaking the swimming night
raising hours to the light
groping for secret images

now lying in darkness and solitude
in chains of the mind locked up
with snows of doubts and reasoning
as his bones of solidness freeze

incerto tempore . . . incertisque loci

is the world
not made of things...
can it be
a magical encounter
between logic and intuition

an abstract mathematical structure
where vibrating grains
of space, time and matter

a higher reality
which is neither matter nor consciousness
where the solid outlines of individuality
melt into a cloud

transient manifestations
of the underlying void

where...

form is emptiness
and emptiness form

is space by itself
and time by itself
doomed to fade away
into mere shadows

holding his head in his hand
suso falls to the ground

i have to abandon
my rational mind
and i have to abandon
all that i know

alas i shall retrieve
the re-written scrolls
i shall nail them down
on the stems of mystery

j now speaks
gently lifting him
from his misery and doubt

in churches and temples
for whom you were looking
is the nearest of the near...
it is your own self

there was a time
when men gave up the gods
and time
the all-destroyer came

and nothing was left
it swallowed up
the saint and the sinner
the king and the peasant
the beautiful and the ugly
he left nothing

suso… she says
the talk that rain makes by itself
all over the ridges …
as long as it talks

you must listen

as it fills the woods
with an immense sound
with insistent and controlled rhythms

you must listen

let it remind you
of all that you've heard tonight
remind you again and again
of the world's rhythms
that you will learn to recognize
rhythms cherished by unintelligible, innocent speech

suso reponds…

these causes…
transcendent objects
for my consciousness
they are outside

in vain

shall i seek to catch hold of them
yet i escape them
by my very existence

beyond my essence
beyond the causes of my acts

j interrupts…

*o' **suso**, many a time*
i have sunk into these bottomless thoughts
and cried out
why has this axe been placed at my root
pitiless spirit
and still i am here
i stand naked on a cliff
and the fabric of night clothes me

in these scrolls
we pass from a world
ruled by reason and the senses
we will pass from infinity
at once definite and bound
to illusions of time and space
in caves of the weary mind
where doubt replaces eternity
and the abstract and indefinite
replace the definite

suso… you shall receive my new scrolls
and when you have read them
and spoken my words
when the people hear

there they will stand before you
they will laugh
they will understand you not
you are not yet
the mouth for their ears

they do not yet
seek a reason beyond the stars

to them
it will be like a puzzle
that can never be finished
with many pieces missing

and the pieces you have given
to them
will not seem to fit

their conception of life
will be as if vanished

o' **suso**

will my written kisses
reach their destination
or be drunk on the way
by the ghosts

i fear...
even the gods are at a loss

never has the penury of knowledge
and vulgarity of sentiment
been so happily disguised

the center has not held
and mere anarchy
is in the process of being unleashed

fratres, agnoscámus peccáta, nostra,
ut apti simus ad mystéria celebránda

XIII

oh, mother of solomon
writer of words
words... censored, distorted and revised
by ancient priests and cultic scribes

to you, he is all too human
he eats, he drinks
loses his temper, is jealous and vindictive
cruel and callous ... methods unimaginable

give us a melancholy lesson
speak to us
we have come to sit beneath your tree
we demand the truth
listening ... we can only imagine what you really mean

we followed you to kenoma
to cosmological emptiness
where we wandered and wept
where the characters are interpreted and meaning is
suppressed

you have rejected all of their judgments
this poem will expose and abandon you
you have imposed your vision on eternity
and commanded that it shall be true

as the night's savagery was
so, your disturbing apothegm
words cradled deep in our hearts

a contempt in the act ... which you have spoken

ah ... but the divine never touches you
and when i too am old
i will dance and strum an oak carved harp
and my words will cast aside this aristocratic idol

and replace the old caustic hucksters
kronos, zeus, yaweh, and hercules
and every idol and image
placing manito loose and allah on a leaf

i hardly know who you are or what you mean
i once walked the old hills of judea
a gentle god by my side
but now, only the squirrels are looking back at me

we stood beneath the last starless night
in empty halls ... on vacant seats
in this place, a once hallowed sanctuary
with no presence ... heaven left empty

where there is a desire not to die
where shakespeare is haunting freud
and mythology leaps into vision
of abandoned paradises...
where faith is shattered and destroyed

but we have finally met ourselves
we are quiet and now stand alone
mother of solomon
you have unmasked the world
you stand in eternal silence ...
your words shall never be condoned

after reciting these verses
los turned to **suso** and explains…

the soul of man
was once moved
through the senses and the imagination
by ceremony and miracle
by myth

he found refuge and solace
in chapels, churches, and cathedrals
in mystic lights and rejoicing bells
in processions, festivals, and ritual

then god was swallowed up
and all the blessed
and the eternal loss of self
and all his unspoken names
came to expire
into eternal namelessness…

los continued in verse…
and did we lose ourselves
as the spirits
were sunken away

four centuries ago
this lofty poem, latin on its crown
where letters have faded…
have the words disappeared
or just turned a discolored watery brown

lost in their superessence
in an unknown darkness

into an abyss
without mode… without form

into an all-bathing ocean of deity
conceived as not a person or spirit
where never was seen the difference
neither father, son, nor holy ghost

yet where the spark of the soul
is more at peace within itself
here…
this formless divinity exists

they both turned to **j**
as she continued to write
she had been writing for the entire night

it was now early in the morning
it was still dark
the sun was about to rise
there was a sound that resonated as she wrote

it was a hum… the sound of **om**
as if nature was telling us
she is pleased with the words of **j**

as they listened
they were propelled into the silence
which was beyond
and all around

the silence was interrupted as **ashu**, now awake
came near… looked down at them
but quickly turned to sit beside **j**

she looked up at his gaze
and with a peaceful expression
began listening as **ashu** spoke…

have you thought
that to retain our ignorance
and fain treat life
as false

where every word is also a mask
as thoughts lie
with the derisive and impartial eye
of an epicurean god

that by putting the vivisector's knife
to the breast of the very virtues of their age
will betray their own secret

shall he then be the greatest
the most solitary
the most concealed
the most divergent

and if our honesty
should one day grow weary and sigh
and stretch its limbs
and they find this too hard
and would fain have it pleasanter
easier and gentler

ah… the devilry we have in us

did the philosopher
come to a stand here

and take a retrospect
and look around

did he here lay his spade aside
and not dig any deeper

to assimilate the new to the old
to repudiate the contradictory

the assortment of new things
in the old arrangements

ah... let us not exist like this
rather let us be becoming
and stand beside
the slowly turning swamp of sounds
with tune and rhythms... with dance

o' you... of whom am i talking to
have i forgotten myself
have i not yet told you of the path

and who shall be this questionable god and spirit
who from childhood onward
has always been on his legs
and in foreign lands

i have also encountered on my path
many strange and dangerous spirits
above all, however, and again and again
the one of whom i have just spoken
i offer in all secrecy and reverence

i have learned much, far too much
about the philosophy of this god

and, as i said
from mouth to mouth
i, the last disciple and initiate

do not repeat what was known
before a weariness of life
even contempt for the present
for the sake of another age

a metaphorical frame
parisian cemeteries
medieval cities in miniature
populated by dead, rather than those who still breathe

death and order
the search for origins
cornered inside an ancient tomb
the conundrum of life... bones staring back

a cemetery's howling wind
muted stone crosses
their book-ended reflection
and i stare below...

the manger now is empty

as if i'd be
hiding in cold and dampness
an uncracked skull is staring back
blasted eye sockets provoking wavering senses
where hamlet stands in contemplation

and all will be discovered as if i already knew

bones unfurled before me

stretched across the centuries
poor yorick, mathematician, philosopher... oh you
jester
your thoughts stand above and outside of me

intersecting the grand, creating the unimaginable
following confusion over their terrains
even poets, priests and philosophers
they stole them, sold them, revered them... who can be
blamed

ashu now turns to the rest

and perhaps i might at last
begin to give you, my friends
as far as i am allowed
a little taste of this philosophy

in a hushed voice
as is but seemly
for it has to do with much that is secret
new, strange, wonderful, and uncanny
as it has been disclosed to me
you are loath nowadays
to believe in god and gods

but such gods do not know what to do
with all that respectable trumpery and pomp
keep that for thyself and those like thee

i... have no reason to cover my nakedness

like numberless humanities
you engaged in their reveling

like a cast of intruders, everything they were wearing
was deceptively tailored in doubt

even thy loftiest thoughts are entangled
and on that day
you stood before them alone...
questioning everything

in this, the chess match with death
you, the one to have the upper hand
having been sent off to la fleche anjou

grounded not in ancient writings
the spirits gave way to you...
thy learned ones
centuries of robed scholars and scribes

convoluted alleys of reasoning
bent in tallow-tapered light
over parchment sheets and leather-bound manuscripts
rubricating, memorizing, parsing and analyzing

strip, erase and let them all crash beneath this holy sea
everything once believed, everything thought to be true
senses deceived, in this cold and stony world... in this
veritable tomb
even things that are standing right in front of you

forces continuing
walls are collapsing
as scales are falling from their eyes
will leave them this cold and stony world...
a grave impatiently waiting

a deep quixotic restlessness
an angry search for answers, for certainty
where once this man stood tall, he lived and breathed
slipped before our eyes… into the dirt and into history

the divide in the universe, the blueness of the sky
the wetness of water
a dance of the sensor and the sensed
this, you bequeathed to the rest of us who came after

with a face like a ghost
suso looked longing at the sea
where once, simpler words
gave comfort to the sufferers
the broken-hearted and distracted
and courage to the oppressed and despairing

ashu continues…
but every word was a mask
as each a supple thought… a lie

cathedrals are
clotting the walls
where they deploy with their bundles
their black robes
their limbs
beyond the obdurate unction of stone

content with tainted dissymmetry

bury them
in the pit of their pestilence

trample them under

to harry the breed in
the sties of contempt of church doors
their monarchial beards
as they explain you away
with a book... of ancient scrolls

mythological explanations
illusion of final causes
arbitrary limits
uninterrupted paradoxes

a refined and complicated play
a difference of degree
deus absconditus
obscurity and incomprehensibility

suso implores **ashu**...

but if we take it away
stripped of distanceless presence
to their world
by the infinite diversity of the roads
and lead them to the object of your world
in its absolute interiority
and by a series of reflective acts
what of the broken-hearted

ashu responds...

i shall exile their dust
and those who contrived them to soil
a contemptable image
till metals remake them
and they issue blaze

like a blade

i then seek to unite them with life
as a magical connection
projected into the heart of the sensation
where the unity of the cerebral functions
is shattered

where phenomena are produced
which simultaneously present a relative autonomy
manifested only
on the rotation of a semicircle around its diameter
here... it finds its justification and its meaning

underneath their apparently logical pattern
their well organized and rational life...
there lies an abyss of irrationality, confusion,
pointlessness
and indeed, of apparent chaos

yes... and i do warn you
it's a dangerous adventure
because they are moving out of the sphere
of their accepted knowledge

so they must jump
and as they now go towards the center
there will come increasingly difficult trials
as if they have to give up more and more
of what they're hanging on to

a total giving up
a yielding all the way

j has heard enough
she gets up and leaves
walks alone in the distance
across the sand... away from the sea
where she enters a dark forest
to sit absolutely alone

to herself she says...

o'**ashu**, not a total giving up
yes, even as with my words...

centuries of robed scholars and scribes
convoluted the alleys of reasoning

but to dismiss the deeper meanings of myth
the archetypes... the motifs as contemptable...
o' **ashu** you have gone too far

from cuneiform tablets to ancient chinese texts
from hieroglyphic writing in the pyramids
to the myths of the sioux
from the most ancient indian texts
to the stories i've told in the bible...
from african stories to those of aboriginal australians
it was all so colorful
as kindly deities created the world by breathing over
abysses

but let us sing with lucretius
where there is no fear of the gods
no ends or purposes in the world
no cosmic hierarchy
no distinction between earth and heavens

but… a deep love of nature
a serene immersion within it
a recognition that we are profoundly part of it
that men, women, animals, plants
and even the clouds
are organic threads of a marvelous whole
amidst an organic, growing
and rhythmically moving cosmos
of a universe in which everything
is fluid and ever-changing

in endless motion
a continual cosmic dance of energy
a great rhythmic process
ceaseless flow of energy

an infinite variety of patterns
that melt into one another
where everything
is connected to everything else

a cathedral
of sapphire eyelids
eternally bowed and gathered
in a tempest of segments

she smiles
as she thinks of the words of **los**

everything we learn about ourselves
in the context of the universe as a whole
reinforces a fundamental fact
that from a cosmic point of view

we are intelligent self-reflective beings

we, i say we
are truly this hidden god
who dwells in the ground of the soul
where the ground of god
and the ground of the soul are one ground
the journey inward
into the dark and silence
is a trip into simplicity

then **los** appears
and as he approaches **j**
he sings…

you are but thy shadow
o' thou loveliest among women
thou hath elevated inward

the wheel of your life
has made its circle
here, the extremes of sublimity and simplicity
are seen to meet

back near the beach
suso walks to the spot where **j** was writing
to the words she has written…

and he began to read

we have seen the ever-changing
ever growing human spirit
emerge from the cave of illusion
and attain the home of the bosom of reality

the fruits of the imaginative genius
upon high levels
to which every self
which desires to rise to the perception of reality
must submit
marked by episodes of splendor and terror
those oscillations of consciousness
between light and darkness

those odd mental disturbances
abrupt invasions from the subliminal
and here lies
the disconcerting glimpse of truth

laid bare to a lucid vision
as our puzzling world of form and color
is to normal light
the hidden child

it lights the alter of every creed

my senses have discovered
the infinite in everything
and as i was then persuaded
and today remain confirmed

where sits a fictitious motif
true meaning escaped
truth now stood reshaped

complexity demystified
the supernatural
has come unbound

i was never created...
that my life begins
is but a masterful delusion
i was the cosmos, a solitary circle

wrenched away from the universe
a piece of life
deliberately broken off
i have become the rocks and trees

the clouds and waters
an intelligible form
of the geometer and architect
a mathematical crystal composed

i will always be living
among blue mountains and green trees
whether straight or curved, jagged or gnarled
a form slightly eccentric and at times out of shape

with splashes and gaps of a roughly stroked brush
interpreting the world
by grasping it, piece by piece
where all are the cosmos

suso reflects on her words
and asks himself
is the winter over
has the time of the singing of birds come

when we will discover
in the folds of a curtain
a figure beautifully drawn
and full of delicate detail

226

all built up out of shadows
that show to other eyes
a different form

he pauses to reflect on her magnificent words
they remind him of the words of a sage
from the mountain and rivers who said...

you have to let go of the self
to let go of that idea
that separates you
from everything else in the universe

realize that the other shore
and this shore
are the same shore
the same thing

ashu turns to **suso** and warns

there is a cosmological emptiness
in which we wander and weep

disbelief is a form
because it is the proof
of another infinity
that isn't its own

the danger ... is that the logic
is not enough to wade in

and if her words
are torn from their context
and presented in a garbled and distorted state
where reality is removed

in this world of imaginative illiteracy

where they wander in the streets
and the birds are silent on his hills
if **j** must go to them
she must go to them as a dancer
instead of mortifying the flesh...
where she lives in her body

but as she walks
her world is not of logic
hers is a world of magic
a world in which imagination reigns

but outside her world
it is a world of logic
where imagination is in decline
and the lower reason attempts
to order life by abstract principles

and the definite replaces the indefinite
and the bound replaces the indeterminate
and reason descends into doubt

and the physical world
takes on the finite character of matter

as **j** labors with bounds
too the infinite... putting off the indefinite
circumscribing and circumscribing
the measureless death about them

remembering all along
the dancer is a plant that responds

to every movement of the water…
to the restricted consciousness of the senses

let not her universe
lose its visionary character
let it not
take on fixed and finite forms

for then they shall know
all along the way
climbing upon false broken words
and false rainbows

between false heavens
crawling and creeping
the brew of fantastic language
and perverting philosophies

those poetic fashions and insanities

can she make them sit still
can she make them listen and understand

that somewhere our unconscious
can yet become as material

somewhere there is a place
where the two ends meet
and become interlocked

and that is the place
where one cannot say
whether it is matter
or what one calls the psyche

the subtle body
beyond space and time

where the distinction between matter
and empty space
finally must be abandoned

the physical vacuum
is not a state of mere nothingness
but contains the potentiality
for all forms
not static and permanent
but dynamic and transitory
coming into being and vanishing
in one ceaseless dance of movement and energy

j steps back into their presence

she proclaims…

yes, to see a world in a grain of sand
and a heaven in a wild flower
that we may hold infinity
in the palm of our hand
and eternity in an hour

when the human spirit is understood
as the mode of consciousness
then, they too shall realize
and feel connected to the cosmos
it shall become clear
that ecological awareness
is spiritual in its deepest essence

i pity
they that sit in the depths of a cave
chained by their ignorance
by their prejudices

where their weak senses
reveal only shadows

they look at a stone
it stays still
but they shall see its atoms
and observe them to be
always now here
and now there
in ceaseless vibration
into a perfect architecture
airy, simple, and extremely beautiful

beautiful, but stratospherically abstract

have not centuries of misinterpretation…
caused the frail unsubstantiated beliefs
to wilt and wither away
leaving a wasteland of doubt

as the scorching rays
of the sun of analytical inquiry
get hotter and hotter
minds disengaged from their moorings

munda cor meum ac lábia mea

as the grey mist subsides
issa moves back within their sight

i have come
to provide a feeling of help
to the helpless
and the comfort of hope
to the hopeless

from the indus river
to ravalpindi
i ran over the pendjab
the land of the five rivers

i visited the golden temple of amritsa
the tomb of the king of pendjab
and turned toward kachmyr
the valley of eternal bliss

descended to the river djeloum
the waters of which flow gracefully
between rocky walls whose tops
reach the azure skies

he pointed heavenward and spoke…

the intelligence and force
which actuate the stars
are inherent with them
and constitute their soul
in precisely the same manner
that intelligence and force are inherent
within the body of man

take, my friends
this is my flesh, this is my blood

as i once provided wine and bread
this, my body
your body
is the body of the whole cosmos

look deeply
and you notice the sunshine in the bread
the blue sky in the bread
the cloud and the great earth in the bread

the whole cosmos has come together
in order to bring to you this bread

acci'pite et namduca'te ex hoc omnes
hoc est enim coepus meum, quod
pro vobis trade'tur

VIV

suso's mind once again drifts back in time
to that time when he as a young boy
was escorted to church each sunday morning

i walked to church
father grabbed my hand
mama sang the moment
i absorbed the meaning

i, the enlightened one
when heaven was young

lined in orderly patterns
everything understood
it was all explained to me
i absorbed the meaning

i the enlightened one
when heaven was young

but this time
there were no angelic guards
rather it is he, that opened his arms wide
and raises his hands heavenward

pater naster, qui es in caelis
sanctificatur nomen tuum

in his mind he was transported
back to the silence, the solemnity

the dignity of the church
and the overpowering atmosphere of prayers
so fervent that they were almost tangible
so powerful that they choked him
with love and reverence
that robbed him of the power to breathe
he could only get the air in gasps

the faint gold fire flashed
from the shadowy flanks
of the upraised chalice at our altar

then **los** stepped forward
and in a hushed tone
said to **suso**

when a man meets god
it is at the point
where eternity intersects with time

it is here… at this very moment
you leave your shells
and at this point you also ask of god
to take off his shells…
those we have put on him

both we and god are to be naked
if there is to be a unification or identity of any sort

in the sphere
in which the natural and the supernatural meet
the dangers of self-deception are very great
some may find the truth in revelations, visions and
apparitions

but most are deceived

now **issa** stepped forward to join them

i have been much misinterpreted by the world
even the most elementary principles of my teachings
have been desecrated
and their esoteric depths have been forgotten
sentences were torn from their context
presented in a garbled state
and thus, a distorted impression

no one today
can know what my thoughts were
or who i am…
who can know

i wrote nothing

but if you read the historical facts
the things they claim that i said
if you read them as metaphors
then you will discover
in a marvelous array
symbols that you can then turn the outer space
into inner space
my ascension
an inward, mythological journey
and the virgin birth
the birth of the spiritual life of each person

if you learn to read the symbols as metaphors
instead of accepting them as the facts
then it will be a source of great strength

it will be your own sacred field

the signs, symbols, language, and liturgy
are an ancient dance
to lift you beyond this bitter world
to a better world

sitting quietly by the sea, was **j**…
she was writing

in the beginning
there is thirst… there is trisnā
feel the world of mysterious forces
the silence in the wet woods

hear the souls of puccini, vivaldi and bach
the winds are howling, the sea is roaring
the clouds of life move so swiftly
and in silence the trees weep

the trees want to see
and we have eyes
they want to hear
and we have ears
they want to bloom
and we have flowers
they want to shine
and we have stars

this fanatic release of the abstract
ideas fiercely wrestling
with never a suspicion
reproduced as if of the ideas of kant

projecting shakespearean hallucinations
pontificating savonarolaesque prophecies
writing laws that rule the harmony of visible form
as if of the form of sounds

it is i, it is you
it is the tree, it is the rock
it is the atom
it is neither blind nor not blind

this wheel of cyclical existence
that has no beginning, middle or end
turns like a whirling firebrand

there is always change
entities are, but momentary
the magical cosmos on full display

the world of origins and destructions
is illusory
when the real world is manifest
so utterly transformed
as if vanished...

the distinction between matter and meaning
or body and mind
or substance and spirit
will be exposed... as an illusion

the sky
the earth and the atmosphere
are woven...
and the wind, together with all life
breathes

the world is constructed
according to our images
there are . . . no eyes, ears, nose, tongue
body or mind

the world is
as a vast flow of events
linked together
and participate in one another

our ultimate nature
is thus a union
between appearances and emptiness
this is the specter of woman and man
the holy reasoning power
and in it, its holiness

the vase is broken
and the scrolls are lost
and shall be re-written and restored
all will be set right

and those grand works
will hold their proper rank
and daughters of memory
will become daughters of inspiration
if we are but just and true
to our own imaginations

bring me my bow of burning gold
bring me my arrows of desire
bring me my spear...
o' clouds unfold

bring me my chariot of fire

alas… what are these…
but, my written and painted thoughts

let us be unknown
let us be knowers
let us be ourselves to ourselves

ah… but you
who have never searched for yourself
how should it then come to pass
that we should ever find ourself

gaze over
beyond this broad and dangerous territory
through which thy mind
has up to this time wandered
the thoughts themselves are older
they have grown riper, clearer, stronger

they have, in fact
grown out of their original shape
and into each other

and from thy answers
shall grow new questions
new investigations and new conjectures…
until at last you shall have a land

and a soil of thy own
a whole secret world
growing and flowering
like a hidden garden

of whose existence
no one could have known

traversing with new clamorous questions
with new eyes
in this immense, distant
and completely unexplored land

you are no longer an artist
you have become rather
the work of art itself

the artistic power of all nature
here reveals itself
to the highest gratification
of the primordial unity
the noblest clay
the costliest marble

you shall be
kneaded and cut
and the chisel strokes
shall accompany you
with the cry of the eleusinian mysteries
as if tossed to and fro
on the billows of existence

yet if you shall go forth
the way shall be opened
through the walls of day
into the dark
where the jewels glow

move here

into your own loneliness
and find the jewel

it's a dangerous adventure
you are moving out of your sphere
into one of detachment and withdrawal
here a radical transfer occurs
from the external

to the internal
a retreat from the desperations
of the waste land
to the realm that is within

there will be a moment
when the walls of the world
seem to open for a second
at that moment you must jump...

then go

to a place directly opposite
of everything you know
everything you've been taught
beyond experiences
to a place...
to a total shift into the unconscious

to a voice
whose sound is like the sea
pure as the naked heavens
majestic, free

where god is not an illusion

but a symbol pointing beyond itself
to the realization of the mystery

acci'pite et bi'bite ex eo omnes
hic est enim calix sa'nguinis mei novi

off in the distance can be heard
the voice of **suso**…
as he sings his words of refrain
remembering those days long past…
when his life was…

lined in orderly patterns
everything was understood
it was all explained
and he absorbed the meaning

he believed he was
the enlightened one
when heaven was young

suso was remember those early days
as a child as he

walked to church
and his father grabbed his hand
his mama sang the moment
and he absorbed the meaning

the sound of the church bells
came to us across the bright sand
where **suso, j, los, ashu, issa and nagarjuna**
all stopped to listen

but, with **suso**

there was something more
than the sound of those bells that attracted him
a kind of interior peace
as he was taken back to that time
he recalls how he loved to be in those holy places
when he had a deep and strong conviction
that he belonged there

it was there
that his rational nature was filled

he now imagined... as if in a dream
that he was back there
he walked in
and looked about the church
and went into a room
where there was a sassoferrato
he stuck his face out a door
into a tiny, simple cloister
where the sun shone down on an orange tree

he walked out into the open
feeling as if he had been reborn
and crossed the street
and strolled through the suburban fields
to another deserted church...
hoping that inside
he would once again find peace
imagining himself wearing the brown robe
and white cord of a friar
and he would be walking in sandals
with a shaved head

in silence
to a beautiful chapel

he stands and bows
imagining he was there
this time, not as a young child

the richness and fullness
came back with a rush
but now he was to enter into it fully

which alone spreadeth out the heavens
and treadeth upon the waves of the sea

we hunger for the spirit
we stand naked, harassed and poor
wearied with conflict
unafraid of death, we stand awed by its mystery, yet
still we remain unsure

the myth and fear and hope
the ceremony and the miracle
never frightened
we have found refuge in the chapel, the church and the
cathedral

in mystic lights and golden bells
behind the façade, burdens are undone
in their courts and palaces, temples and schools
we kneel before the virgin... we are transformed by
desire and the darkened sun

he knelt
or rather now threw himself down

before pietà in the cloister corner
and buried his head
in the huge sleeves of his cowl

solemn psalmody
their prayer flexed its strong sinews
and relaxed again into silence

and suddenly flared up again in a hymn
the color of flame
and died into silence
and he could barely hear his weak
ancient voice saying the final prayer
the whisper of the amens
that ran around the stones like sighs

ashu then interrupts **suso**
as if awakening him from his blissful state
and warns...

there are truths
which only possess charms

where the gulf between knowledge and capacity
is great and mysterious

born... enemies of logic
and of the straight line

ah... i will take you back
back to a time
when our ancestors became at last
transfigured into gods...
the very origin

perhaps an origin from fear

then… the conqueror of god
and of nothingness
unreality and falseness
of his innermost being
that he then
sometimes attempts to trespass

on to the most forbidden ground
of reality
here he attempts to have real existence

the thorough un-switching
of the human soul
the plunging of it into terror
into frost, ardor and rapture
so as to free it
as through some lightning shock
from all the smallness and pettiness of unhappiness

what if nothing proves itself to be divine
unless it be error, blindness and lies
what if god himself
proved himself
to be our oldest lie

but only with that ideal's outworks
its outer garb, its masquerade
with its temporary hardening, stiffening and
dogmatizing

it is rather one of the final phases of its evolution
one of its syllogisms and pieces of inherent logic

it is the awe-inspiring catastrophe
of a two-thousand-year training in truth
which finally forbids itself the lie
of the belief in god

and just as the muses
descended upon the dull and tormented boeotian
peasants
so, philology comes into a world
full of gloomy colors and pictures
full of the deepest, most incurable woes
and speaks to men comfortingly
of the beautiful and the brilliant
the godlike figure of a distant blue

i once crawled in terror across a narrow ridge
where the flame was guttering and rough
and tortured shadows stared back...
fed ill-famed teachings of narrow and rigid formalism

where talk of absolute truth and authoritarian dogmas
were imposed in tyrannical religio-mystical drama
which are... but fleeting phenomena
of a vast, unknowable, infinitely connected thus-ness

suso cries forth

i returned
now you have torn me away
from the scents... the hidden and forgotten treasure
the drop of goodness and sweet spirituality
and even my dream-night thoughts
from all experience of my own

and the world's divine ground

ashu retorts

under thick dark ice
is a divining-rod
for every grain of gold
long buried and imprisoned in mud and sand

suso… in a pleading response

the genius of the heart
now richer in myself, newer than before

and you now have broken it up…
blown upon
and sounded the thawing wind

leaving me more uncertain
perhaps, more delicate
more fragile, more bruised

i am fearful…

ashu somberly states

what as yet you lack
you know not what

in a hushed voice… **suso** proceeds

as is but seemly
for it has to do with much
that is secret, new
the fine ceremonious
the tides of luster and merit

i shall, in this instant
extol my courage
my fearless honesty, truthfulness
and love of wisdom

i no longer have reason
to cover my nakedness

j steps forward, chastises ashu and responds...

alas, only birds have now strayed
and fatigued by flight
let themselves be captured with the hand
with our hand

these, my written and painted thoughts
for which alone i have colors, many colors
perhaps, many variegated softenings
and fifty yellows and browns and greens and reds

but nobody will divine thereby
how ye looked in your morning
your sudden sparks and marvels of solitude

let doubt not turn against itself
doubt in doubt

yet, i shall allow no one to read the new scrolls
to know these scrolls
unless every single word therein
has at some time wrought in them
a profound wound
and at some time exercised
a profound enchantment

then and not till then
can one enter the joy
of participating reverently
in the halcyon element
from which this work is born
in its sunny brilliance
in its distance, its spaciousness
and its certainty

but to you, o **suso**
the whole inner world
originally as thin as if it had been stretched
between two layers of skin
has burst apart and expanded proportionately
and obtained depth, breadth, and height

and imprisoned as you were
in the oppressive narrowness
and monotony of custom
in your own impatience
lacerated, persecuted, gnawed
frightened and ill-treated

only by diving, burrowing
and penetrating into reality
will you at once, be taken back
by these means... to the redemption of this reality

ashu now protests

but let us, forsooth, my philosophic colleagues
henceforward guard ourselves more carefully
against this mythology of dangerous ancient ideas

which has set up a pure, will-less, painless
timeless subject of knowledge

let us guard ourselves
from the tentacles of such contradictory ideas
these theories an eye that cannot be thought of
is required to think
an eye which ex-hypothesi
has no direction at all
an eye in which the active
and interpreting functions
are cramped, are absent

if i am in any way a reader of riddles
then i will be one with this sentence
for some time past there have been no free spirits
for they still believe in truth

has indeed any freethinker
ever yet wandered into this proposition
and its labyrinthine consequences

that stoicism of the intellect
which eventually vetoes negation
as rigidly as it does affirmation
that wish for standing still
in front of the actual, the factum brutum

this renunciation of interpretation
of forcing, doctoring, abridging, omitting
suppressing, inventing, falsifying

what if this belief becomes more and more incredible

it makes the life in the ideal free once more
while it repudiates its superficial elements

j responds

as the poet is incapable of composing
until he has become unconscious
and reason has deserted him...
the mythical figures
have to be the invisibly omnipresent genii

under the care of which the young soul grows to
maturity
by the signs of which the man gives a meaning to his
life and struggles
and the state itself knows no more powerful
unwritten law
than the mythical foundation

and now the myth-less man
remains eternally hungering among all the bygones
and digs and grubs for roots
though he has to dig for them
even among the remotest antiquities

the stupendous historical exigency
of the unsatisfied modern culture
the gathering around one of countless other cultures
the consuming desire for knowledge

what does all this point to
if not to the loss of myth
the loss of the mythical home
the mythical source

the fundamental understanding
by all those who are in search…

in search of a path
in search of a direction
in search of a meaning
in search of themselves

they will become wanderers
they cannot remain static

perhaps god too
is the ultimate excuse for wandering
perhaps …
you will never find him
your wandering will remain eternal

is this the beauty of god
that you can long for him
but you cannot find him…
that nobody has ever found him

but in all this wandering
in all this searching
in all this mountain climbing
what do you find
you find only yourself

opening into one's deeper nature
is like surrendering
into an ocean of presence
far vaster than you ever imagined yourself to be
abiding in the gently pulsing stillness

let this be
the core of thy being

allusive, elliptical
and cryptic language
that pierces the knot of duality
the dense part at the base of a flower
between the fire and the poison

the scriptural corpus
of the entirely unpublished

beyond language
wordless

ashu responds... the world has been de-sanctified
myth deities personify energies that are around us in
nature

things are connected like the blood which unites us all
man did not weave the web of life
he is merely a strand in it

j interrupts... i have walked up and down
in the history of time

when arm'd clouds arose
and even my senses were shaken
fanatic struggles
profound dissensions
this sharp line of demarcation
is it magic or religion
do they mean the same

dare to trace them to their origin

magic… the crude aggregate
that paved the way for believing
a slow and continuous thought
overcome by solitude
surrounded by invisible dangers
and claims of the absolute

i have entered a new realm
one not of living things
i now live in the rhythm of spatial forms
where all i feel and see, i am imagining

back to the world of myth
in the balance of light and shadow
into the confusion of fantasy, the original chaos
filling the gaps with what we cannot ever know

i spoke, but my words had lost their meaning
i saw people coming towards me
but all were the same… all were myself
i had never known this world until today

experience the very cosmos
as you experience your own body
a magnified projection of what is happening within
you
where a deception of symbols pretend to be reality

there is a secret place inside this world
where they make transactions with beauty
where the pattern of time is lost inside of you
jiggle the key until it turns smoothly

until, in the course of innumerable ages

even the grass, the rain and the dust
wear their disguise
and you awake beyond the boundary of your own body

ashu then states
yes… and you watched
as man has walked in perilous paths
into barren climbs
to worship from poetic tales

of such harsh terror
has driven me to madness

yes… remember jonah
the fish's nostrils
so wide to draw in… even the ocean

j, did you not write such stories
will man's eye discern the flying cloud
and knowing the artful secrets
the stories
leaving them fearful, cautious and trembling

even this day
refusing all definite form
the abstract horror you penned

even the horses are mad
harrow's confounded
companions enraged

tightly kneeling in their churches
as the king of their theater
in full regalia

with pomp and inspiration

genius forbidden
by laws of punishment
from them they make an abstract
which is a negation
of the substance from which it is derived

yes... their heavens and their inhabitants
their blood of punishment
hid in soft slumberous repose
hid from the terrible east
trembled in death's dark caves
in cold despair
terrible combustion clouded rage

j, *your words stand pale*
they stand around the house of death
in temptations and despair
among the rooted oaks

if error be removed
reason, not on both sides
shall walk among the stones
of fire... in bliss and woe

till two eternity's meet

like a mandrake in the earth
before reuben's gate
giving a body to falsehood
that it may be cast off forever
the land of darkness flamed
but no light

and no repose

the land of snow is trembling
and of iron hail incessant
the land of earthquakes
and the land of woven labyrinths

every universal form
has become as a barren mountain
and every minute particular hardened
into grains of sand

and all the tendernesses of the soul
cast forth as filth and mire
among the winding places
of deep contemplation

intricate among the ruins of the temple
and vala who is her shadow
clothed in black mourning
upon my river's currents

o' **j**
you talked with the grey monk
as you stood in beams of infernal light
and a harlot that is what you were
sold from street to street
defaced with blows
bleeding in torrents
from mountain to mountain

all the while
you thought you glittered
with precious stones and gold

but what they saw
were garments of blood and fire

in vain
you hurried afar into an unknown night
where even the sun and moon
raged in the conflict

o' chemosh, o' bacchus, o' venus
o' double god of their generation
the heavens cut you like a mantle

you wept in deadly wrath of the specter
in self-contradicting agony

but now, these altars run with blood
their fires are corrupt
their incense is a cloudy pestilence
all the while playing in the thunderous loom

in sweet intoxication
filling cups of silver and crystal
with shrieks and cries
colored vapors
before the eyes
of the divinely dissatisfied one

it has been disclosed to me
you are loth nowadays
to believe in god and gods

each one is the farthest away from himself
and you and your band
are no longer knowers

the joyous confidence
that once spilled ink on those scrolls
neither separate disconnected capricious
nor sporadic phenomena
have but sprung from an uncommon root
a fundamental fiat of knowledge
whose empire reached to the soul's depth

among a quarter of the earth
and who's words grew
ever more definite in its voice
and more definite in its demands

the origin of evil already haunted me
at an age when games and god
divided their hearts

but o' how hostile
to the kantian article
and how pregnant with abominability

XV

off in the distance
near the sea
a loud piercing scream was heard
it was a fight
between a leopard and eagle...

after a lengthy battle...
the leopard prevailed
the leopard carried its prey
to a secluded area beneath a tall tree

he did not go unnoticed
his adversary, the spotted tiger
pounced forward
the two engaged in a desperate fight for the bird's
lifeless corpse

they fought and fought...
they fought to their own death
as they lie dead
their blood soaked the earth beneath the tree

the blood nourished its roots
and in amazement
the tree's leaves began to expand
their color deepened
but the weight caused the branches to weaken

the leaves began to bleed
first a deepened red

then the color faded
turning to a glowing white

as the leaves fell
solid forms emerged
with letters engraved in an unknown language

los stepped forward
as he and **suso** together
began piecing the images together

suso's smile widened
as he proceeded in his attempt
to place the words of the scrolls
in their proper order

everything eternal
is but a metaphor
mythologies might be defined in this light
as poetic expressions
of just such transcendental seeing

los speaks

order and life
the modifications of chaos
and meaning as well as value
are both a human creation...

this belief can both serve to liberate us
for new acts of creation
and to paralyze us
with a despairing acknowledgement
of the emptiness of life...

a deduction that must be disguised

man has created through his imagination
another world
a fantastical world of refuge
against the suffering in this world
against the fire that burns him to ashes

los then took his leave
and walked toward and into the water…

suso upon hearing these words of **los**
advanced toward the tree
and gazed before it with a wearied look

ah… but have i been born young
have i been born too soon

if i wished to shake this tree with my hands
i should not be able to do so
but the wind, which we see not
troubleth and bendeth as it is listeth

yet they are sorest bent
and troubled by invisible hands
as soul is bent and tormented
most by invisible hands
by unheard speeches
by doctrines or interpretations
that permeate our perceptions

the tree
rooted in life
cannot escape from its place

and its life is surely badly twisted
and badly treated by the wind

los steps toward **suso**
thereupon, **suso** peered into his eyes
disconcertingly

los continues…

it is the same with a man as with a tree
the more he seeketh to rise into the height and the
light
the more vigorously do his roots struggle earthward
downward into the dark and deep

as the tree connects with the two worlds
the branches grow heavenward
through the lifegiving air
and the roots are nourished
with the juice of the earth

today this nourishment is with
the blood of these beasts

still perplexed
suso looks with a look of confusion

los explains

so, the effort is
to transcend the outmoded
or decadent standards
and thus create the new

and you, o **suso**

you… presently remain
in an incomplete stage of thy awareness
the tree symbolizes a life
that is utterly strange to the mind

when the tree appears
it receives nourishment
directly from the blood of the beasts
and a new form of life appears
another type of life which has not known before

in this sphere
the natural and the supernatural meet
here, the dangers of self-deception are very great

here some may find the truth in revelations
visions and apparitions
but most are deceived

turning to **j** who was still standing near…
suso in a look of despair, asks

has thou discovered my soul

j steps back, with the slightest of a smile
steps forward to respond

many a soul one will never discover…
just as the quest of the knight errant
who seeks the holy sepulchre

you, in courage and bravery have sought
the treasured words from the broken vase
and today
as the leaves turn a brilliant white

and fell to the ground
as if wanting to speak

but no one could understand it
but you, **suso**, have entered this
and witnessed the changing color
and the fall from above
from blood-red to bright white…

suso asks…
are these the words of the scroll

but **los** interjected

it is as if
the sea was tied to the tree
and half the world was sand
the other half mercury and the sleeping sun

but you didn't come to see the sky
rather you came here
to see the muddled blood
that sends blood-red scrolls to the waterfall
and the spirit to the cobra's tongue

los placed his hand on **suso's**

and trusting to his guide
suso followed him among things undisclosed

in the distance
he heard strange languages
words imbued with rage and despair
cries rose in a coil of tumult
noises like the slap of beating hands

fused in a ceaseless flail
that churns and frenzies that dark and timeless air
like sand in a whirlwind

and **suso**, with his head in a swirl of error, cried

what is this i hear
what people are these
whom pain has overcome
the sorrowful state

suso look into the sea
he could barely make out
people as if upon the distant shore

it seemed by this dim light
that all were eager to cross over

suso asked

who they are
los answered…
these and many more are things you will discover

los walked toward the water
stepped into a boat
his white hair blew against the wind
there appeared sighs that trembled the timeless air

suso saw a fire
that overcame a bleak hemisphere of darkness
turbulent in a storm of warring winds

los resumes
i am the old man

and i surface seldom

but you, o **suso**
you will come in with the tide's coming
when seas wash cold
and all obscurity stares with a danger

it is then
that you shall ravel to clearness
on the dawn sea and muddy rumors

for the archaic trenched lines
of your grained face
shed time in runnels
aged and beat like rains
on the unbeaten channels of the ocean

you will unwind the labyrinthine tangle
to root deep among knuckles, shinbones and skull
inscrutable, below shoulders
not once seen by any man

you will defy questions
you will defy other godheads
you will walk dry on your kingdom's border
in the murderous thick air
you will breathe the water

j steps forward and speaks...

is something more beautiful in shape
in color so resplendent
is something of more worth
beyond where the words stretched forth

and are fallen from the tree

that i should hold it to thy ear

suso raises the words to his ear

and heard that instant in an unknown tongue
which yet he understood
articulate sounds
a loud prophetic blast of harmony
an ode, in passion uttered
the song in which the calm look declared

the voice
the one that held acquaintance with the stars
and wedded soul to soul
in purest bond of reason
undisturbed by space or time

a god…
yea many gods
had voices more than all the wind

with power to exhilarate the spirit
and to soothe
through every clime, the heart of human kind

while these words were uttered
strange as it may seem
suso wondered not

he plainly saw
one to be as a stone
another a shell

it is here... at this very moment
you leave your shells
and at this point you also ask of god
to take off his shells
if he has any...
except those we have put on him
both you and god are to be naked
here there is a unification
in the sphere
in which the natural and the supernatural meet

the dangers of self-deception are very great
some may find the truth in revelations, visions and
apparitions
but most are deceived

he thus attends the motions
of the viewless winds
embodied in the mystery of words

there, darkness makes abode
and all the host of shadowy things
work endless changes... there
even forms and substances are circumfused

suso reflects once again on his childhood experience
when he left his boyhood faith
because of his dismay
as they discarded
the beauty of ritual
and sacred language
they had forgotten
to send you out

rather they wrapped you back in

they took you
from multi-colors to colorlessness
from the color of the clouds
to the colorlessness of the moon

then a time came
a terrible time
when you were dragged through the void
into the presence of this new and different god

where the words
were spoken in lines unhallowed
devoid of the once sanctified

how it hurt
burned the eyes, ears... all of the soul

these agonizing thoughts
tortured during these years
corrected only by doubt
and fear and sadness

it was in the midst of these gloomy shadows
in those stifling nights
that every moment
seemed to intensify

entrapped
whirling thoughts rushed in my mind
i could make nothing of them
sentences were left unfinished and obscure
sometimes an overwhelming heaviness

was laid upon the earth and upon my soul

and when the great murmuring had died away
and the air had ceased at last to quiver…
here i knew nothing around me
in me everything was changed
my god was no longer…

so, my days were now spent
in a series of unbridled outbreaks
from dread and fear
to an endless fall into emptiness…
a furious wind in the desert

cracking the very bounds of my existence
my thoughts filled the sky
the universe, space
the world coursed through me, like a cataract
in the horror of this cataclysm

suso was swept along
by the whirlwind
which brushed away
and crushed like straws the laws of nature

he was breathless
he was drunk with the swift hurtling down of god
god–abyss
god-gulf
fire of being, hurricane of life… madness of living
aimless, uncontrolled, beyond reason
for the fury of living
he sought the solitude of the fields

and delivered himself up to it
drank his fill of it
like a maniac who wishes not to be disturbed
by anything in the obsession of his fixed ideas

j then took his hand
and in the great sweet air
in contact with the earth
his obsession relaxed

he abandoned himself
to the forces, newborn in him
to the absurd
grief, pity, despair

the aching wound of an irreparable loss
all the torment of death
that could only sharpen and kindle into being in the
strong
as they rowel their sides with furious spur

wretched is the sterile creature
that man or that woman
who remains alone and lost upon the earth
scanning their withered bodies

and the sight of themselves
from which no flame of life will ever leap
wretched is the soul
that does not feel its own fruitfulness

j spoke to him about a new day…
a week, a month, a year
it didn't matter

he will then be permeated with imagination

sometimes it will take shape in an isolated phrase
complete in itself
more often it will appear as a nebula
enveloping a whole world

the structure of the image
its general lines will be perceived through a veil
torn asunder here and there
by dazzling phrases which stood out from the
darkness

with the clarity of sculpture
then it will disappear again
into its mysterious retreats
leaving behind it a luminous ray

what was it

nagarjuna, who had listened to **j's** words intently
stepped forward and spoke…

suso, the truth is the same for all of us
but each of us has its own lie
which it calls its idealism
every creature therein breathes it from birth to death

it has become a condition of life
a few will break free
through heroic moments of crisis
when they are alone
in the free world of their thoughts

dusk was falling

nagarjuna said, come with me
they walked together along the beach
and there over across a road
was what appeared to be an abandoned church
they went down into it
where the dark shadows
were creeping along the gigantic walls
in which the magic eyes of the windows were shining

like two circling worlds
they had passed close to each other
in infinite space
and now they sped apart
perhaps for eternity

as the artist must show his universe
which never was and yet will ever be
they came to what seemed to be
the depths of the ages
where **nagarjuna** now confessed to **suso**...

in the silence of my solitary life
to the forest filled with birds
i, like the monk of the legend
slept in the ecstasy
of the song of the magic bird
the years passed over me
until... after day, months... years
the evening of life was come

suso, while he listened
stepped into a vague dream
in which music replaced the words

and made him forget them

until, at once he spoke…
to whom can i pray

at this moment he had to pray
he had to pray within his soul

nagajuna spoke…
only the weak of spirit never needs to pray
they never know the need
that comes to the strong in spirit
of taking refuge
within the inner sanctuary of themselves

pray **suso**… you must pray

suso… got up and turned to leave
to walk back along the beach
alone with his thoughts
as he left behind
the mysteries of the day
in the vivid silence of his heart
the waters of his solitary life
stirred and shifted above him
and never touched him

he heard the blood beating in his veins
beating like an inward voice, crying
like whitewash trickling down a wall
under the beating of the rain

but… his thoughts turned again to the scrolls

were they forever lost

will **j** reveal them to me
only to be remembered as a secret
which should only be murmured
in the silence of the heart

nagarjuna rejoined him
through the sandy path
on the ocean-side…
they did not speak

suso mused sadly
as they walked along
close together
there was silence in the wet woods

and in silence the trees wept
from the depths there came
a sweet plaintive cry
of a solitary bird
who felt the coming of winter

as **suso and nagarjuna** returned

los now spoke

o' **ashu**… o' **suso**… o' **nagarjuna**
was not **j** the one to herald
and announce the adventure
through its often dark, loathly
and terrifying path
and so often judged evil
by the world

the gates of understanding

often closing so fast

but… as you go towards the center
many have missed the aids
they were not prepared
for the increasingly difficult trials
even giving up more and more
of what they were reaching for
and hanging on to

and in the end…
a total giving up
a yielding all the way
a failure to move toward that
of which they knew nothing
where the deeper you go
and the closer you get
to the final realization
the heavier the resistance

here is where one discovers for the very first time
that there is everywhere a benign power
supporting him in his passage

but just as in the sun
objects paint their images
on the retina of the eye
so they, sharing the aspirations
of the whole universe
tend to paint
a far more delicate copy
of their essence in the mind

like a metamorphosis of things
into higher organic forms
is their change into melodies

over everything
stands its daemon
and, as the form of the thing
is reflected by the eye
so, the soul of the thing
is reflected by a melody

all the gods of the world
are metaphors, not powers
do you think that jesus was god…
was god's son

yes, he was… and we all are

tat tvam asi

XVI

los continued

listen
and look carefully
arouse in your mind
a sense of awe

you will discover
yourself in the rites and symbols
though they have been distorted
and have become alien

do you insist on reasserting the holy writings
as historical fact
instead of the symbols of the heart and spirit
thereby distorting and debasing

when the language of metaphor is misunderstood...
its surface structures become brittle
its spiritual signal
if transmitted at all
becomes ever fainter

if we give that mystery an exact meaning
we diminish the experience of its real depth

there is great strength to be gained
by letting go
by going beyond
beyond your plane of being
letting the rituals propel you

out of the quotidian quagmire
into a transcendent transposition
into another realm

ashu steps forward and says to **los**…

if her archangel now, perilous
from behind the stars
took even one step down toward us
our own heart, beating higher and higher
would beat us to death

who does she suppose we are
early successes
creation's pampered favorites
mountain-ranges, peaks
growing red in the dawn

flowering godheads
joints of pure light
to corridors, stairways, thrones

who, if i cried out, would hear me…
her words have consumed me
in my overwhelming existence

yet her heroes and gods live on
even in their downfall
they are merely a pretext
for achieving some final birth

they are real in the hearts and minds
of a quarter of the earth's people
and their joints of pure light

their corridors, stairways and thrones…
space formed from essence
and shields are made of ecstasy

and from the mountain top and the pulpit
all things conspire to keep silent about us
half out of shame perhaps
and half as unutterable hope

sometimes i find that my hands
have become aware of each other
or that my time-worn face
shelters itself inside them

invoke that hidden
guilty river-god of the blood
erect and summon the night
to an endless roar

the halls are filled with suspicion
and this restless future, delayed for a while
is adapted to the folds of the curtain
into strangling undergrowth
prowling bestial shapes
to ravines where horror lay
still glutted by the holy fathers…
and every terror knew them

winked like an accomplice
yes, atrocity smiled …
the fathers now lie in our depths
like fallen mountains

dried-up riverbeds

of ancient saints
a whole soundless landscape
under the clouded sky of its destiny

he now turns to **j**...

o' **j**, dear children reach out to touch your holy words
flowering and fading have come to them both at once

and, troubled by the aftertaste of thy unfocused gaze
as if the suburban sky had wounded the earth

the unconscious gaping faces
deaf and sometimes a little confused
as if in widowed skin

fate, which is silent
suddenly grows inspired and sings
into the storm of his onrushing world
what voice can outshout the rattle
of this drained and broken age

by the rising and falling of ancient fountains
lest you squander their hours of pain
and then you gaze beyond them
into the bitter duration
to see if they have an end

imagine that they no longer walked
through their grief grown wild
no longer looked at the stars
through the jagged leaves
of the dark tree of pain

o' **j**... is this what you have to give

boys, too sharp at the edges
although perhaps sometimes skillfully cut
like pieces of rock
that have fallen on flowers

a shelter nailed up
out of their darkest longing
with an entryway
that shudders in the wind

at bottom
the ancient one
gnarled root hidden deep
origin unbeheld by those who branched up

possessed by shadows
with illness near
and you will let their blood flow darkly
as they wrestle and rage

and each one of the sharp stones
that they hurled
vengeance-crazed
lest they kill you
and break you in pieces
while your words keep lingering on

the surface
is perpetually giving way
before one
and revealing another surface below

dissolving as it is touched
this making of holy words

melting into the making of the earth

fading into an allegory
of the rising and the setting of the sun
accessible
but incomprehensible

j responds…
ashu, how many regions in space
have already been inside me
there are winds
that seem like my wandering son
do you not recognize me
air, full of places i once absorbed
you who were the smooth bark
roundness, and leaf of my words

how much was once gazed
into the charred slow-dying glow of fire
those glances of life, irretrievable

who knows what losses
i have suffered
once more the rhythm of men
through the held-back silence
of the resolute
into the silent seamless world

so, **ashu**… let not one god pass away
we all need each of them now
let each be valid for us
each image formed in the depths

don't speak with the slightest disdain

of whatever the heart can know...
everything breathes in accord

ashu responds...

how tracelessly they have gone away
those cares of the night
where darkness was formed
in pure contradiction, from your legions of light

the existence of the terrible
in every particle of the air
you breathe it in
but within you it precipitates, hardens
acquires angular, geometrical forms in among your
organs

for all the torments and horrors
suffered on your altars
in your temple chambers
under the arches of bridges in late autumn

all this is possessed
of a tenacious permanence
all of it persists
and jealous of all that is
clinging to its own frightful reality

wouldn't the masses
prefer to forget
sleep each motif away
gently... at the grooves in the brain

but you won't let them

even in their dreams… drive it away
and lines anew are retraced
and they wake, panting

and dissolve the gleam
of a candle in the dark
and drink in the half-lit solace
estranged to thyself

like a shadow on water
that moves through a corridor of fathoms

i sped through the exile
of each man's existence
this way and that
and so, to habitual loathing

for i saw
that their being was this
to stifle one half of existence's fullness
in an alien limit of ocean

and there, in immensity's mire
i encountered their death
death gazing the barriers
death opening roadways and doorways

if only it could have mantled the whole world
and an angel led you out to that solitary desert
out through the mountains of the wilderness
where the kings and courtesans and anchorites lie at
rest

and there he would have sprung

aloft and away
fearful that you would begin
writing anew
believing then, that your mighty spring
you would have poured forth
unheard, giving back to the universe
what only the universe can endure

but he stands there
like a candle burning down
the remainder of the wick still glowing
warm through… and never moving an inch

and how it is that he still tempts and entices them
is beyond anything that the many witless little birds
can judge

you could not wait for this life virtually
without spatial substance
condensed by the centuries into drops
and at that, his powers have given out

the two ends that you had bent together
have sprung apart
and his mad strength
fled the willowy wand

and it was as if
your work had never existed
your scrolls torn and scattered
in a period of despair

and then with such vehemence
your god took on form

and then shattered
almost in the same instant

i dreamed that instead of a bride
he was given a naked sword
i imagined that what you were looking for
might suddenly break forth from within me

or that my ears should burn
and my hands be cold as metal
or that a tall candle beside me
should burn right down to its holder

with every line you wrote
you broke off a portion of the world

life is assembled
things vibrantly intermingle
and move out into the air
and their coolness makes the shadows vivid

all things are everywhere
and one would need
to be a part of it all
if nothing were to be missed

i knew at once
that your image of him was valueless
the absoluteness
was but of his misery

mitigated by no wariness
and no role-playing whatsoever
was beyond the power

of even my imagination

i had understood
neither the angle at which he was bowed to
nor the terror inside his eyelids
that seemed continually to fill him

the fateful thing
about those dramatic poems
was that they were forever amplifying
and extending themselves

growing to tens of thousands of verses
so that at length the time represented in them
was real time
much as if a globe were made on the scale of the
earth

the concave stage
beneath which was hell and above which
representing the level of paradise
a balcony of unrailed scaffolding

attached to a pillar
merely served to undermine the illusion

but now o' **j**
you are out into the wide open
and there is a sense of disconcertment in the air
and even your walk is unsteady

j falls to her knees
turns heavenward
tears flowing in the sand

and she prays

will you never again tell me
o' sound and breath of the air
will you never again tell me
disturb the forest, roads, spikes of grain
mist, the cold

have everyone of your footprints
been incessantly consumed

say someday
you will let me go
from star to star
until i reach the rain's nest

and your ocean
bring me a day
embracing your waves

what's waiting for you
where, without hallways
without walls
like a plainsman you hear the earth's cup
in your hand

you put your ear in the roots
from afar a wind
from a fearsome hemisphere
where the needle stitches time
with fine water

has it become disjoined
has the seam disintegrated

or is it all ash
mere hope
developing my eyelid...
only blood

the spill on a leaf
here, from the noise of a gallop
the water goes wounded to earth
without fight

in splintering star-shaped, moonlike, icelike
a cyclone of horses
riddled in my pain
with points like an icicle prism

my outcry, moving shadows, grinning shapes
sorrows, terrors, laughter, dreams, dreams ...

all was a dream
i am where all light is mute
with a bellowing like the ocean
turbulent in a storm of warring winds
a hurricane in perpetual motion
sweeping twists and torments
driven as if to land
reaching the ruin... groaning, tears, laments

it is time some genius should appear
to reconstitute my shattered picture
to live in the continual presence of all experience

nagarjuna appeared before **j**
then spoke sofly...

o' j… queen mother
only the gods have written about you
yet, this day
there are collisions, beneath the shore

elliptical thoughts
and terse turns of phrase are striking
with saccadic gestures
and sentences punctuated with silence

vague abstractions
sentences thrown out in bursts
erosion of old and new
juxtaposed action and dream

and now
your thought digs down into thought
finding only emptiness

i shall take you deeper
deeper into your very thoughts
your very actions and perceptions

if you are the pattern
of time's orderly passage
do not go
but if you do
you must wear a disguise

if there is self-existence
apart from the basic elements
where a dreadful world appears

is it here

that all phenomena arise
dependently upon other phenomena
as if... momentary atoms of experience

does what we call change
occur in but a series of moments

if so
then reality is something different
from the input we receive
and different form the way the mind speaks
in each silent moment

when the mind is quieted
and the multiplicity of things disappear
are all things
and events perceived
interrelated and connected...

are they all just different aspects
of the same ultimate reality

come with me
to see the world
this system of inseparable, interacting
and ever-moving components

where you, my dear one
are the observer being
and an integral part it all

withdraw into the forests and mountains
meditate upon the order of nature
and observe...

sit motionless and observe

here the concept of empty space
loses its meaning
where form is emptiness
and emptiness is form

thus, attempt to confine
the fluid forms of reality
in fixed categories
created by the mind

where the false notions of a separate self
have forever disappeared
and the oneness of all life
has become a constant sensation
the dynamic aspect of all phenomena
the ceaseless transformation of all things

let your mind's eye create worlds
where there exists
an entity diffused throughout space
where between you and me
there is a lake
of vibrating lines
that transport your image to me

where images
are not constructed by the external world
where consciousness becomes one
with all that you see

where atoms
at the center of the stars

feed their fires
and form interstellar molecules

and the primordial oceans
and the interwoven helices
of you and me
are ideally suited and embroidered

a hundred-billion neutrinos
are streaming
through our bodies every second

particles that aren't fundamental
but are vibrations
of infinitely small strings of energy

j responds…
never before have i felt so sure
of ancient times
i can almost smile at those generations
that wept for antiquity
as for a lost play
they would have liked to have parts in

now i grasp the dynamic significance
of that early unity that was in the world
that new and simultaneous gathering

it will not trouble them
the readers of my words
that that civilization
which was all of a piece

i will now appear to them

to the many in later ages
to form a whole
and to be wholly past

los now stepped forward... and said
they will behold the dark tranquility
the diamond flowing water of your voice

he then stripped a branch
to make a flute
he threw a stone and watched it
ripple across the water
he stooped to the ground
obliged a beetle to turn around

and the heavens passed over
as if merely passing over nature
almost as though she had a soul
but, as a matter of fact
she only borrowed one

suddenly over the moor
reached great shadows
the air was still
and life seemed to withdraw
into the veins of the earth

only the music of the flute
went on calmly
sounds bubbled forth
like springs from all the corners of her soul

and from every stone of the roads
by which she walked

j passed into a magic world
and in her heart
there was a strange, mysterious emotion
the dream of humanity wrapped her
about the strange flowers of the soul ...

wide horizons
vast plains over which the mind soars
and is lost

a river with gray eyes
gowned in pale green
hearing the voices
and the silence of all things

the stillness of it
the harmonious dullness
the monotony
has a charm for them

and a sweet savor
which cannot be analyzed
which they malign, love
and can never forget

walking bare-foot on the cool sand
and on the dewy turf, and on the stones
cold in the shadow
burning in the sun

and beyond the path from the beach
was a little stream
that ran along the outskirts of the woods

then **nagarjuna** said to **j** these words…

you have been lifted to the stars
and hurled down to the depths of hell

be silent, say nothing, listen …

slowly the creaking of the axle-tree of the world
shall die away
and the rumbling over the stones
of the heavy car of action
will be lost in the distance

and there will arise the divine song of silence …
the hum of bees
and the perfume of the limes …

the wind
with its golden lips
kissing the earth of the plains …
the soft sound of the rain
and the scent of roses

there will ring out
the hammer and chisel of the poets
carving the sides of a vase
with the fine majesty of simple things
solemn and joyous
with its flutes of gold
and flutes of ebony

pressed on into mysterious recesses
of the world of hearing
discovering new lands

in that inward ocean

thinkers, who, with supple
and many-sided minds
emulating the endless...
a flow of moving things

go on ceaselessly trickling and flowing
staying nowhere
nowhere coming in contact
with stubborn earth or rock
and depicted not the essence of life

even after a thousand efforts
when you have climbed half-way
and can climb no farther
being held bound
in a dull and difficult existence

while in secret
burning away in obscure devotion
lower still, at the foot of the mountain
in a narrow gorge between rocky crags

the endless battle
the fanatics of abstract ideas
and blind instincts
fiercely wrestling

with never a suspicion
that there may be something beyond
above the wall of rocks
which hems them in

still lower
swamps and brutish beasts
wallowing in the mire
and everywhere, scattered about the sides of the
mountain

the fresh flowers of art
the scented strawberry-plants of music
the song of the streams
and the poet birds

but only you can perceive and hear
the silent music of their souls
most hear it not

the silent calm of the motionless sea
the stormy, troublous depths of their own soul
i cannot separate
thought and form
like the stove of descartes
from which the suppressed ideas
darted upward
to the free sky

to worship a god
you must become a god
and find in yourself
the level of conscious and love
that the deity epitomizes and symbolizes

when you do
you are worshiping that deity

when avalokiteśvara looked down

upon this suffering world
he was filled with such compassion
that his head burst into innumerable heads

while from his body sprang
a thousand helping arms and hands
like an aura of dazzling rays
and in the palm of each hand
there appeared an eye of unimpeded vision

he appears to brahmans as a brahman
to merchants as a merchant
to insects as an insect
to each in the aspect of its kind

the power of a deity
is that it personifies a power that is in nature
and in your nature

but **ashu**
it is as if you have fled from life
drifting along in a world of poetic fictions
that had no body
no flesh and blood
no relation to reality

but men who are weary in soul
recoil from life
they can only bear to see it
through the veil of visions
spun by the backward movement of time

no doubt
you have discovered

the profound meaning
of those years of trial
where each test was a barrier
which was burst
by the gathering waters of the river

a passage from a narrow
to a wider valley
which the river would soon fill
to a wider view and a freer air

o' **ashu**
i found and hazarded in my mind
the most diverse answers
that you have established
in these distinctions in periods, peoples, and castes

but isn't this
just a temporary shutting
of the doors and windows of consciousness
the relief from the clamant alarums and excursions

through the growing fear
that they exercise on the imaginations
and now have grown themselves
into monstrous dimensions
and become relegated to the gloom
of a divine mystery
that transcends imagination

but you, **j**… in you
there is in a strain of innocence
which rings out in the distance

like the sound of invisible bells
over there, over there
on the other side of the horizon

i know
you don't always understand it
sometimes it comes
wafted on the wind…
it comes from where you do not know

and then it disappears
as strangely as it comes
the mystics and the saints
did not see things as they were
they imagined them
through the prism of desire or regret
they seemed
to be peering through the chinks
of the old wall

but, like you
they knew much more
they knew all the things
which you too are longing to know

and they clothed them
with sweet, mysterious words
which you have been appointed to unravel
with infinite care
to find the secrets of the heart

there are many lights and shadows
in which you want to be left in peace

with the unvaried rhythm of the universe
planets moving through space
mingling its chorus
with the harmony of the spheres
alone together in a submissive universe

but there is, but one soul
among multitudes... among millions
each one as different...
different as the worlds moving in the heavens

it is the same flash of thought
which lights up their hearts
though the centuries divide

in that dark room
in which the images take shape
an order of mind
where the senses thrill
in answer to every puff of the winds
and when the light of an old faith dies down
it is met to salute the kindling of the new

to him as to them
the world was not
an incoherent collection of reasons or facts
but an infinite space
steeped in darkness
and quivering with light

while through the night there passed
the beating of mighty wings
all bathed in the sunlight

how many voyages of the mind
one can make
standing up with wide-open eyes

to many are the defects
marked and exaggerated
the wings of faith have been clipped
and left dangling over the abyss
without understanding
of the hidden forces
in the river

and **suso**
that you could recover the memory
of your childish dreams

but in your sorrow
nothing could be clearly seen
but great moving veils

thousands of streams, currents and eddies
twisting into form
then fading away
like the blurred procession
of mental images
in a fevered mind

forever taking shape
forever melting away

over the river's murmur
filling the darkness
with its eternal muttering

that was far more sad
than the monotony of the sea
broken in soul and body

you, like a storm cloud
rumbling in the darkness
with the plaything of an illusion

where the connection lies only in words
words that outrun the reality of life

cold reflections
of the lights falling from vanished suns
stars that have been dead for ages

but to me, there is
outside the instincts of species
the cosmic force
which is the lever of the world

that openest the abysses of the soul
thou dost destroy
the normal balance of the mind

the doors are opened
the demons appear
and, for the first time
the soul sees itself naked

o' **suso**…
you became like a dismantled hulk
rolling rudderless
at the mercy of the winds
in vain did you try to escape

you strove mightily

has thou worn yourself out
in the attempt

or has thou
found thyself
brought back to the same place
as if shouting to the wind

to receive its eloquence
truth must be spoken in unveiled form
in throbbing, dancing trees
and swirling, starry skies

gracefully amid the rocks
where crystal waters flow freely
where at first every wave's an outsider
before it disappears into itself

become one with this ocean
come close to the center
let the great silence descend over you
enter the interior world

let doubt be your pilgrimage
something is there, something unexplainable
ask every question
ask... but not a solitary answer will be known

simply sit silent without thoughts
an oceanic consciousness now surrounds you
here the two polarities dissolve
and all contradictions meet

XVII

suso speaks…

i once crawled in terror
across a narrow ridge
the guttering flames
were rough and tortured

shadows stared back…
fed ill-famed teachings
form was narrow and rigid

authoritarian dogmas
absolute imposed drama
mystical drama
vast and fleeting… but unknowable

substituting and disguising
that inveterate practice

what deceit to misappropriate pictures
of present delight
in order to sell them behind our backs
to heaven

where my heart
resembled that forgotten chapel
and a temple garment
was thrown over me… but never inside

los spoke…

suso, you have carried off

the uncertain music
sandals removed
in infinitely connected thus-ness

yet, the quiet of the senses
in infinite interdependence
with no conceptions
layered onto it
revealed a timeless connection

yet... ragged lines form above the horizon
where chaos burns through the egyptian darkness
like an allegorical shadow-show
that vanishes the moment the light is kindled

a picture held you captive
all your thoughts and feelings had fallen away
until an unknown sensory world appeared before you
naked
where ancient myths and mysteries were unveiled

now beholding what begins and promptly ceases
in a life of quiet contemplation
in an unfolding narrative beyond the realms of
thoughts
beyond a transcendent and unknowable consciousness

then... strong and wide
there you were
spreading to reach
with a thousand roots deep into life

and, through sorrow
grew far out of life

far out of time

now… peer through this
our imaginary world
just sit
suspend all judgment
here in warm waters…
and simply, calmly flow
in this not-knowing

what you call the most correct
the systematic
and mathematical language
of the present time
and the hazy, mystical
and mythological
language of the ancients

yet they differ
only in clarity…
buried in nuggets
behind these myths of truth

suso responds to **los**…

after long searches
in temples and churches
on earth and in heaven

at last
i came back to my own soul
completing the circle
from where i started

to find that he whom i have been seeking
for whom i have been weeping and praying

yet when i painted god
nothing happened

but i know that i have a poetic self
that constantly turns into other things...
falcons, storms, songs, trees, ships, sandals
and that also
turns god into those things, too

i believe in all that is as yet unspoken
i wish to free my most pious feelings
that what no one yet has dared to say
will one day come naturally to me . . .

i shall go to the mosque
i shall kneel before the crucifix
i shall enter the temple, where i shall take refuge
i shall go into the forest and sit down in meditation

the ascetics wander shrine to shrine
looking for what can only come
from visiting the soul

i shall study
the mystery that embodies me

in this
my groping mind
holder of the external
i shall believe in a river-god
a sky-god

a cloud-god
a rain-god

where is it to go
where is it not to go

my childish dream
this puerile illusion of birth and death

los agrees and continues **suso** thoughts

of heavens and higher heavens
of lower worlds

all vanish

birth and death are in nature
not in you

one millionth part
simply sits down
and says
we are all god
o' ye men
o' ye animals and living beings

the whole world has been changed
in half an hour

take away the self
and the universe vanishes

go through smoke
then to night
then to the dark half of the moon

there is nothing that is not god
it may frighten you
but you will understand it by degrees

and yet men search churches and temples
and believe imaginary things
through ceremonials and forms
in a journey from truth to truth

j appears
tired and worn
she confesses to **suso and los**…
tonight, my words fail me
phrases elude me
where once they tripped nimbly
at my command

my thought, alas, dies
before it reaches the point of my pen

los responds…
then prepare to put the pen aside
and let the further pages
be written on water
let the curtain of silence
fall upon them
direct your thinking inward

and **j** did thus…

floating swiftly
in a boat with a huge sail
under a strong breeze
down rivers and streams

riding slowly
in the saddle
on a plodding beast

driven
up the old highway
silver sheen glittered
over the white dust
that lay so thick upon the road

on whose edge she walked
where shadowy robed figures
passed her in the night
sometimes with dancing lanterns
sometimes with bowls in their hands

she once stepped into utter solitude
lived alone with wild beasts
of the massive forests
the lofty deodar trees
and the snow-clad giants

in which all things live and move
of which they and she
are but a single expression

j turns toward them… and speaks

o' **suso**… o' **los**… o' **ashu**

we shall find god
at the end of this quest
as he really is

neither the glorified man

nor the attenuated gas of metaphysics
rather in its utter stillness

in this manner
we are forever and inseparably dwelling
in the realm of the present

as the essence of our existence
defies observation
and is completely unknowable
in a timeless absolute
which lurks behind
the scenes of our thoughts

see the infinite in all things

if the doors of perception were cleansed
everything would appear
as it is… infinite

and you o' spider
if the spin of your web
were fast as light
as an iron chain…
it would be
yes… the solid and the hard
the state of matter…
the spinner of the night
through the void and the empty

you are the river
of unbroken streams
changing
every particle

in a state of flux

a mighty river
rushing to the ocean
and all the drops
that constitute your stream
being drawn
to that boundless ocean

there is something in you
wanting to fly beyond
where the body cannot follow
but which is chained

you can't jump out
you can't go beyond

this continuous fight
against the laws of nature
go inside
there too is the fight going on
between light and darkness

where the manifestation
is always changing
revealing more and more
of the reality behind

yet, through all of these
runs the golden thread…
discover this thread

this standing between
the known

and the unknown
in this mysterious twilight
the mingling of the truth
and of the false

the pleasure and pain
and a thousandfold more

we come here weeping
to fight our way
to make a path
through this infinite ocean

long ages behind
an immense expanse beyond

to solve the mysteries
there arises
the wall of beginningless
and endless time

a few steps
a wall of boundless space
particles of matter
irrevocably bound
walls we cannot go beyond

the vibrations and motions
the delusion of permanence
the rapid succession of thought
the delusion of matter
in succeeding waves and hollows

if we can find the beginning

we can find the end
if we find the end
we can find the beginning

intelligence unfolding upon itself

use the word
cleanse it
and realize fully
the material
and the efficient cause
in the minute cell
and all that evolves
at the other end

and it becomes god
slowly unfolding his nature
becomes the lowest atom
rejoins himself

a whirling, combining, mingling
mass of change
a tossing mass of waves

where few have a glimpse
of the calm sea behind
i believe in all that has never yet been spoken
in these swelling and ebbing currents
these deepening tides moving out and returning

i will confess you
i will announce you as no one before has

i was there with the first mythmakers and monks

who made up your stories and traced your runes
but now i see you
winds, woods, water, roaring at the rim

nagarjuna appears before them
and says… you and i
the sun, the moon, and the stars
are just different names
of different spots
ocean of matter
an ocean of changes

the particle of matter
was once the sun
today… it is you
tomorrow a plant
ever coming and going

one unbroken, an infinite mass
differentiated only
by names and forms

this universe
but an ocean of thought
rising and falling

yet man has closed himself up
the rays of light
enter his eyes
yet there is no vision

even as forms emerge
and new suns, moons, and stars
watch the shadows that are cast

scarcely beholding the great light
conversing with the void

space is silent
when we let time stand still
when we transcend the ordinary mind
in that place where meditation becomes a mystical
poem

slow down the movement
no longer fear the silence
transmute your part of this cosmos
beyond the one-dimensional

deepen your understanding
create your destiny in every moment
enter the mind-field of ahamkara
now, close your eyes...

let your thoughts embrace the rain...
its pattern of geometric complexity
do not deny the myriad of forms before you...
let yourself gaze intently on yourself

the universe is an ocean of energy
listen to its sound
its vibration pervades a world immovable
even as the earth meditates alongside you

then **j** says
the anguish of those who advance
must advance slowly

you must not absorb the scrolls too quickly

as your today will contradict your yesterday

things which enter
and depart from matter
are but imitations of being
and semblances catching at the shadow

but the scrolls
re-written and read by the mind
once merged with the sea
and disappeared into the unknown night

yet the mountains will not have fled…
for the western gate of the city
the gate of the sense
is never closed

next n**agarjuna** says…

because we cannot understand
the real
we end up lost in confusion.
that which we call the material world
is still a representation inside our brains
a fusion of mind and matter.

i turn myself
into a star's vast silence
above the strange and distant city…
of time

growing ripe upon your vision
as upon a tree
from the sloping threshold

slowly, lift one black tree
and with that, the world is made

… all abstractions
abstractions as reality
exist only in these thoughts

the huge, many leveled, many colored life
the innumerable words which escape the rhythm of our
senses
a divinity
a greatness of destiny

far beyond
a physio-chemical theory
your own birth is not your past
and your own death is not your future

the only real time is now
in emptiness there is no form

abstract and concrete are fused into one…

los adds…

i went into utter solitude
living alone with the wild beasts
in massive forests…
the lofty deodar trees
and the snow-clad giants
which towered overhead

i let body and mind
slip into the most quiescent state
shrouded in mystery

rooted in obscurity

i came to know
the essence of things
the illusion of forms
where finite is attached to infinite

i found consciousness
shivered to atoms
under this expansion of nothingness
enclosing the absolute in a limited space

where form
is an error of your senses
and substance
an illusion of your intellect

so come
let us sit together
cross-legged
sit beside me... make your mind easy

experience the seven solitudes
without measuring reality
without differentiating the written
from the painted thoughts

j looks into **suso's** eyes
she sees his questions...
his need for answers as she says to him

the incarnations from the symbol to its reality
from the letter to the spirit
from the hand-built exterior sanctuary

to the unwrought unshaped interior stillness

we will know fully by insight
the essence of the tiniest creature
to the essence
of the whole universe

the mind-essence
is as much present in a piece of stone
as in an animated human being

hence when i wrote the words of genesis...
and the earth was without form and void

there was no movement
no activity in it
yet it contained the endless possibility
of all movement and all activity

from nothing comes everything
from silence all sounds
from unconsciousness emanates consciousness
from zero all numbers
from invisibility everything visible
and from intangibility all that is tangible

this seeming nothingness
is the secret basis of the whole universe's existence
undimmed by mists and uncovered by illusions

give up the dualistic
the greatest fallacy
behold the matterless principle
the unknown god

the most mysterious element
in our mysterious existence
left trembling on the verge of a bottomless chasm
which it is forever unable to cross

suso...
through your various wanderings
and woes
you shall recover the ruined empire
of your soul

its passionate immortal energies
and gate-keepers
that govern dreams
and the flight of birds

they pass through
the rays of the whole
of our sight

by their rarity
reverberate them by their splendor
and escape them by their subtlety
cloud, wind, sky and ocean
even they are... spiritually animate

when men and mountains meet
as if a voice were in them
motionless as a cloud
yet the old man stands
and hears the lone winds as they call

then you too, o' **suso**
you must hold infinity

in the palm of your hand
and eternity in an hour

and you will hear
the cries of birth
a voice
throughout the universe

wherever a grass grows
or a leaf bud
the eternal man
is seen, is heard, is felt

was it god
that you saw
did you see him sail away
out of our site
as the sun-beam fled
from the sea

suso replies

flying as a bird to the upper world
… in a trance beyond all bounds
passing from the sphere of waking consciousness
… beyond dreams, between all thoughts

i will dance as the rain falls upon my face
as the hactin paints the mounds of sand before me
where distinction between life and death is dissolved
here… i will meet the mysterium tremendum of the
unknown

where i will hear a thousand voices reply

and hear the forest tremble
see animals and plants as indistinguishable
in a world of form... in a world of emptiness

i shall worship the sun
if the sun does not exist
i shall worship nature
and if nature does not exist
i shall worship the stars

j steps forward
looks deeply into **suso's** eyes

today you have listened
you have found my words
the scrolls... my little book

you must eat them
let them become sweet as honey inside of you
and thus, they will have been found
within you

dominus vobiscum
et cum spiritu tuo

Index

A

abandoned 42
abbreviated inspiration 155
absurd 134
achilles 40
adonis 170
aeneid 42
ahamkara 351
allegorical 339
alleys of reasoning 240, 244
alpha and omega 171
alter 167
alter the cosmos 76
a lyrical poem 139
amitābha 152
amphitrite 101
anagnoristic 168
analyzing 240
andromeda 136
anger and meaningless 47
apocalyptic 154
apollo's face 101
aquinas 45
arbitrary meanings 199
archetypal dreams 164
aristocrats 81
armour of diomedes 39, 123
ashram of silence 114
a treasure king's land 221
attached to nothing 197
attis 170
augustine 43

authoritarian dogmas 272, 338
axis mundi 168

B

bach 260
bagdhad 135
barbaric 46
beauty 81, 134, 165, 166, 216
beyond all bounds 358
beyond all dimensions 197
beyond the boundary 220, 221, 281
blasphemed 81
blasted eye sockets 238
blessed 78, 167
blindness 166, 182
boccaccio, 44
bodhidharma 150
bodhisattva 74
book-ended reflection 238
bottomless ocean 120
boundless ocean 198, 203
broken 42, 101, 132, 134
buddha 123

C

calumet 169
canons of logic 35, 76
carbon 135
cathedral 163, 165, 169, 269
cathedrals 81, 100
central mountain 168

uninterrupted paradoxes 242
universe 86, 124, 134, 135, 136,
        137, 165, 171, 240
unknown sensory world 339
unraveling cascade of life 97
unsettled 86, 164
unstable isotope 137
unsympathetic wave 87
untouched 120
untrammeled 139

V

vainglorious communiqué 81
vengeance 41
venus 101, 102
veritable 240
virgin 78, 269
vivaldi 260
void 96, 120

W

waking consciousness 139, 358
way of dragons 151
whimsical protons and cells 127
white-gloved majestic 46
whitman 48
wisdom 123, 167
within time 74
wounded king 169
wretch 183
wretched 167

Y

yahweh 43
yearning 168, 182, 183
yorick 238

Z

zeus 42

9 781643 887